MELODIC MINOR GUITAR COOKBOOK

Master the Melodic Minor Scale & Add New Depth to Your Guitar Solos

JAMES **BUTLER** & JOSEPH **HOSKIN**

FUNDAMENTAL**CHANGES**

Melodic Minor Guitar Cookbook

Master the Melodic Minor Scale & Add New Depth to Your Guitar Solos

By Joseph Hoskin and James Butler

Published by **www.fundamental-changes.com**

ISBN 978-1-78933-207-0

Copyright © 2020 Fundamental Changes Ltd.

The moral right of this author has been asserted.

All rights reserved. No part of this publication may be reproduced, stored in a retrieval system, or transmitted in any form or by any means, without the prior permission in writing from the publisher.

The publisher is not responsible for websites (or their content) that are not owned by the publisher.

www.fundamental-changes.com

Over 11,000 fans on Facebook: **FundamentalChangesInGuitar**

Instagram: **FundamentalChanges**

For over 350 Free Guitar Lessons With Videos Check Out

www.fundamental-changes.com

Cover Image Copyright: Shutterstock – Mervas

Contents

Introduction	4
Get the Audio	5
C Melodic Minor	6
D Dorian b2	14
Eb Lydian #5	24
F Lydian Dominant	31
G Mixolydian b6	39
A Aeolian b5	47
B Super Locrian	54
How Do We Use This?	65
Further Reading	78

Introduction

Welcome to the 'Melodic Minor Cookbook!'

In this book we will take you through the seven modes of Melodic Minor and show you how to use them in pop and rock music. We believe that pop rock guitarists in general could benefit from knowing more about the Melodic Minor modes, and while they are commonly associated with jazz music, they can be effectively used in other styles of music. The purpose of this book is to add to what you already know by incorporating the Melodic Minor modes into your playing.

Each mode of Melodic Minor contains a number of intervals that are unique to that particular mode and distinguish it from all others. We refer to the distinct intervals as the 'sweet notes' of each mode, and by identifying and targeting these notes; we have a recipe for bringing out the 'flavours' of the mode.

Our goal is to teach you how to use these 'sweet notes' to bring out the desired effect in your soloing; break away from the conventional scales, and put some spice into your playing. We have prepared detailed explanations, reader-friendly diagrams, and examples that will help you understand the Melodic Minor modes. This book comes with a selection of backing tracks to help keep it fun and familiar.

While you will learn about the Melodic Minor modes, the focus will be more on their application and how to incorporate them into your existing knowledge, rather than the theory behind them.

This book will have you cooking with the Melodic Minor modes in no time; people will be amazed with what you do in your solos.

Let's show people that jazz isn't the only place you can go to hear a mix of spicy licks and smooth phrases.

Get the Audio

The audio files for this book are available to download for free from **www.fundamental-changes.com** and the link is in the top right corner. Simply select this book title from the drop-down menu and follow the instructions to get the audio.

We recommend that you download the files directly to your computer, not to your tablet, and extract them there before adding them to your media library. You can then put them on your tablet, iPod or burn them to CD. On the download page there is a help PDF and we also provide technical support via the contact form.

www.fundamental-changes.com

Over 11,000 fans on Facebook: **FundamentalChangesInGuitar**

Instagram: **FundamentalChanges**

For over 350 Free Guitar Lessons With Videos Check Out

www.fundamental-changes.com

C Melodic Minor

1st Mode of C Melodic Minor

Using the Melodic Minor mode is a great way to break out of using conventional minor modes like Aeolian and Dorian. The Melodic Minor mode can be thought of as the Dorian mode with a major 7th. This means that we are using minor 3rd, major 6th and major 7th intervals. Although traditionally associated with minor/major7 chords, the Melodic Minor mode can also be used over minor7 chords

Mode Positions

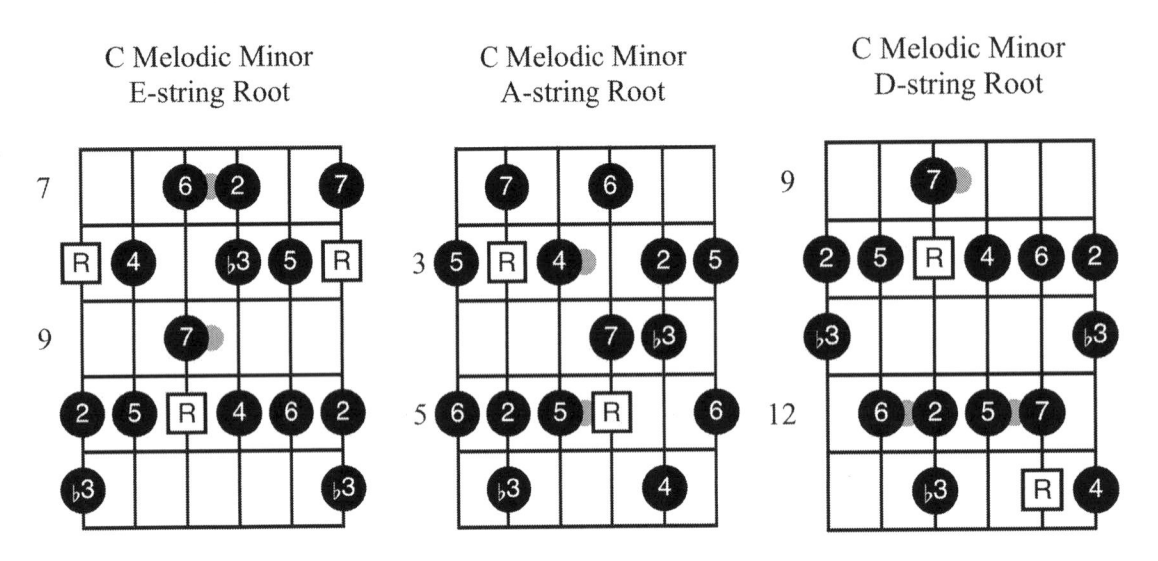

Practice these patterns to familiarise yourself with this mode. Play these shapes over the minor/major7 and minor7 chords.

Chord Diagrams

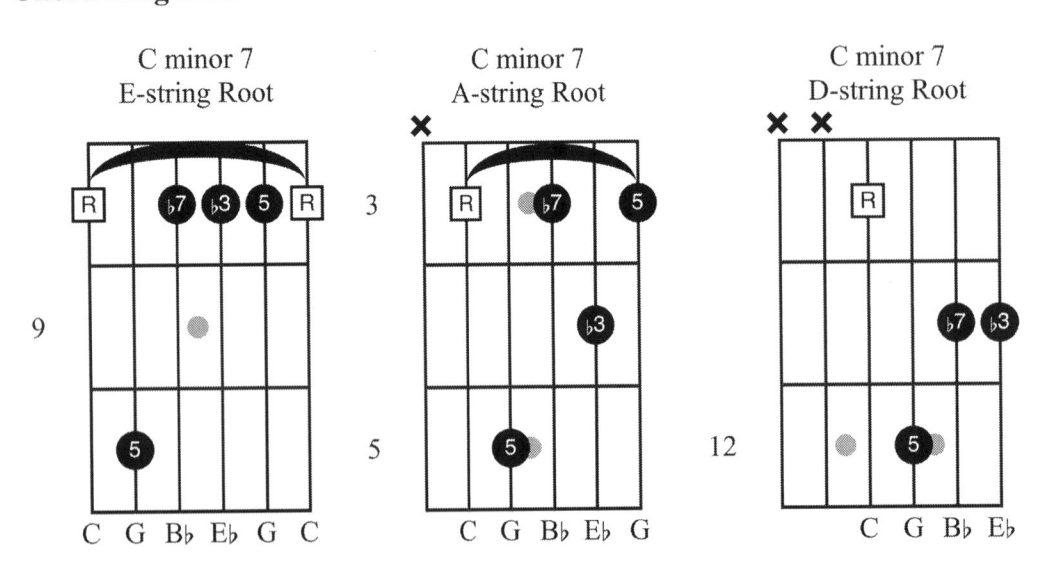

The Melodic Minor mode can be used over minor/major7 chords because they both contain minor 3rd and major 7th intervals

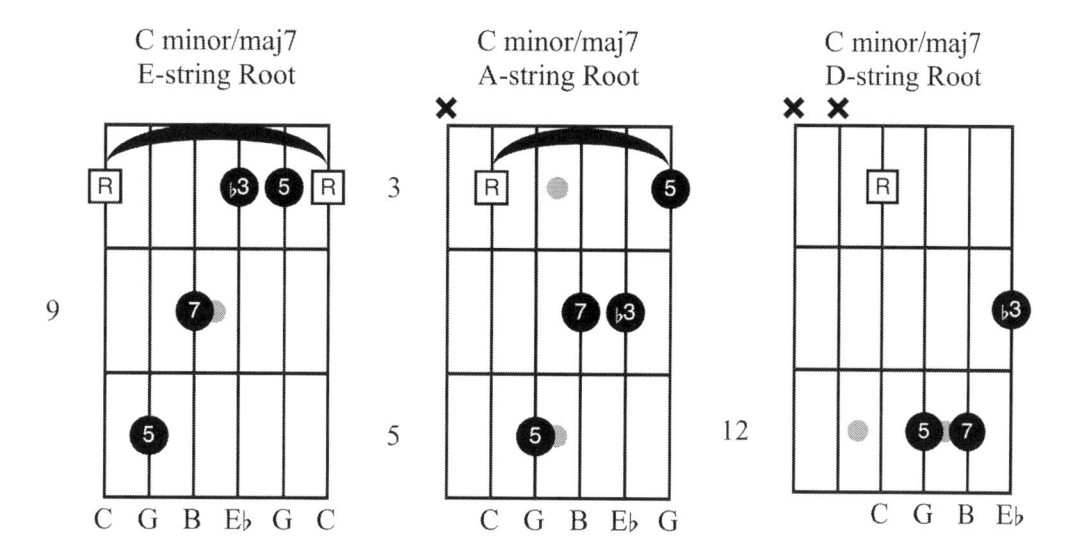

[Chord diagrams: C minor/maj7 E-string Root, C minor/maj7 A-string Root, C minor/maj7 D-string Root]

Although the Melodic Minor mode has a major 7th, and the minor chord has a minor 7th, this does not negate the minor quality of the mode, instead it adds some tension.

Cooking With Arpeggios

The next thing to do to become familiar with the sound of the Melodic Minor mode is to play the arpeggio. In this case, the arpeggio focuses on our 'sweet notes': the minor 3rd and major 7th intervals.

Food For Thought

These arpeggios can be used effectively at the start of a phrase in order to establish the Melodic Minor sound.

Here are some C Melodic Minor arpeggios:

Example 1 | Track 1

This is a C Melodic Minor arpeggio in root position being played over a C5 chord. The 'sweet notes' in this arpeggio establish the Melodic Minor sound.

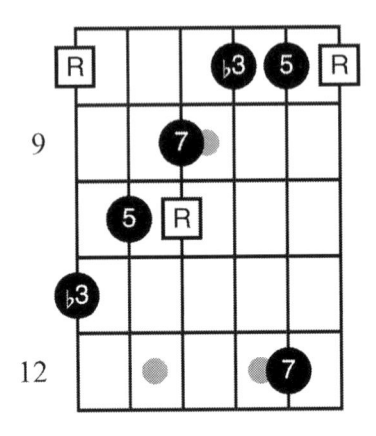

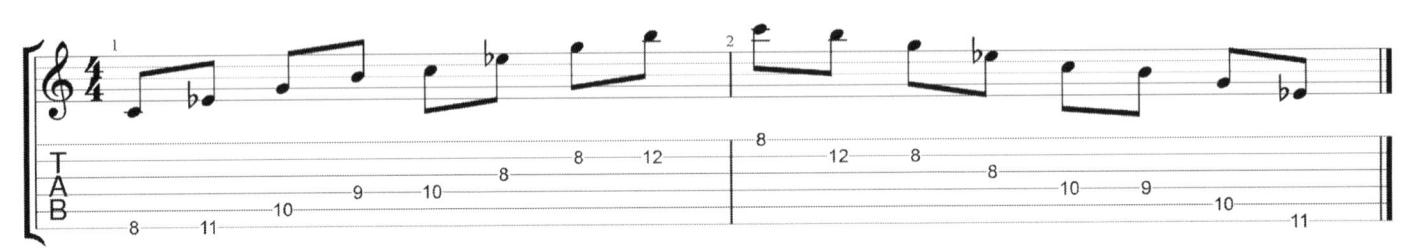

Example 2 | Track 2

This shows is a C Melodic Minor arpeggio in 1st inversion being played over a C5 chord. This will help you play Melodic Minor in different positions on the fretboard

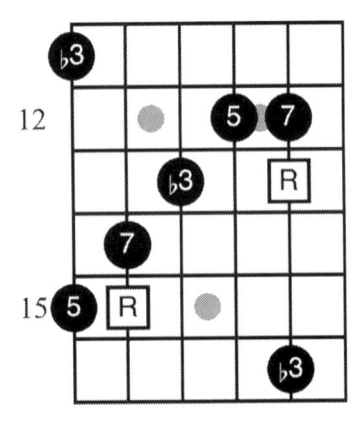

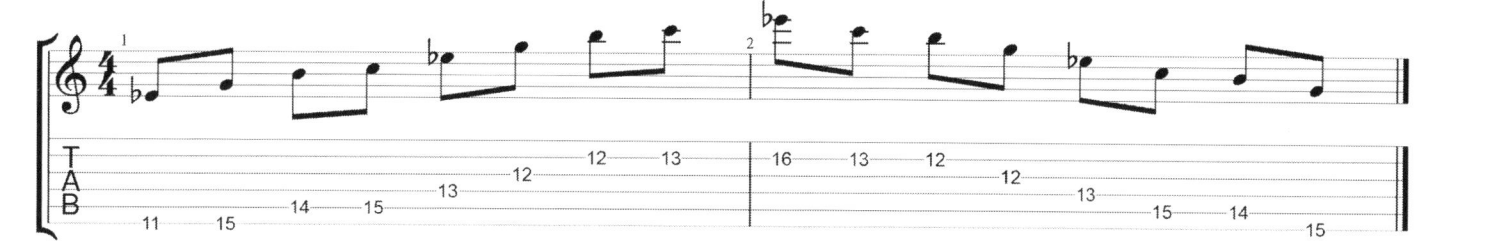

Example 3 | Track 3

Here is an example of a C Melodic Minor arpeggio in 2nd inversion being played over a C5 chord. This one is difficult to play, take time to play this one clean.

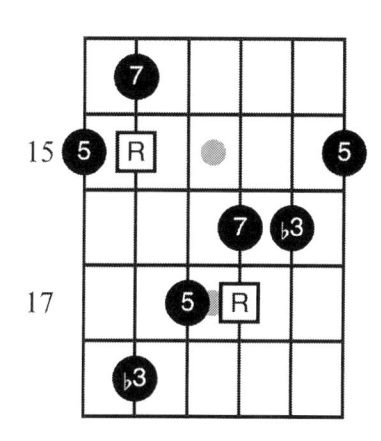

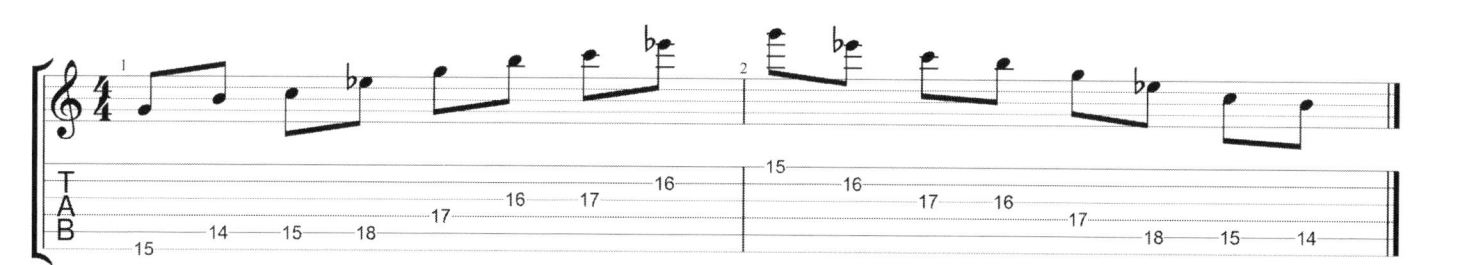

Practice these patterns over the backing track provided at the end of each example. Use these arpeggios as starting points for writing your own solos.

Targeting The Sweet Notes

Every mode contains a certain combination of intervals that distinguishes it from every other mode; these are what we refer to as 'sweet notes'. The trick to further understanding the Melodic Minor modes is learning how to utilise these intervals.

As we mentioned before, the 'sweet notes' of the Melodic Minor mode are the minor 3rd and major 7th intervals. By basing licks and runs around these two notes we can clearly hear the tonal qualities of the Melodic Minor mode.

These are some examples based around the minor 3rd 'sweet note':

Example 4 | Track 4

The minor 3rd is an easy note to set up due to it often being present (or at least implied) as part of the chord we are playing over. This example is resolved to the major 6th, A.

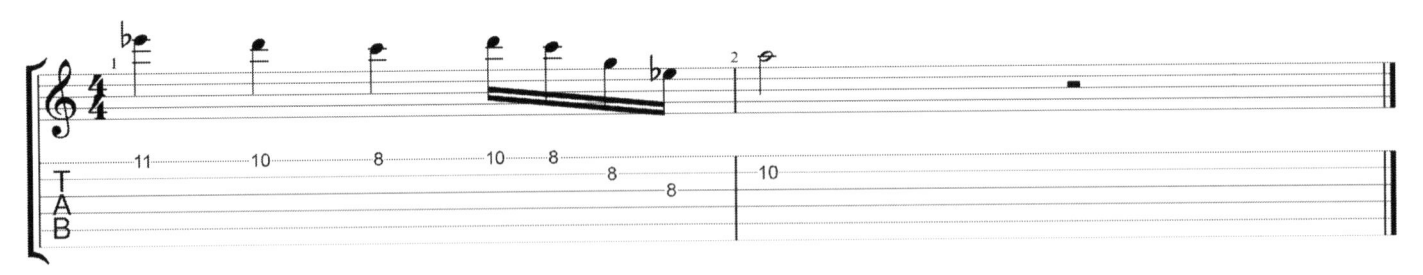

Example 5 | Track 5

This is resolved to the 5th. See 'home notes' in glossary.

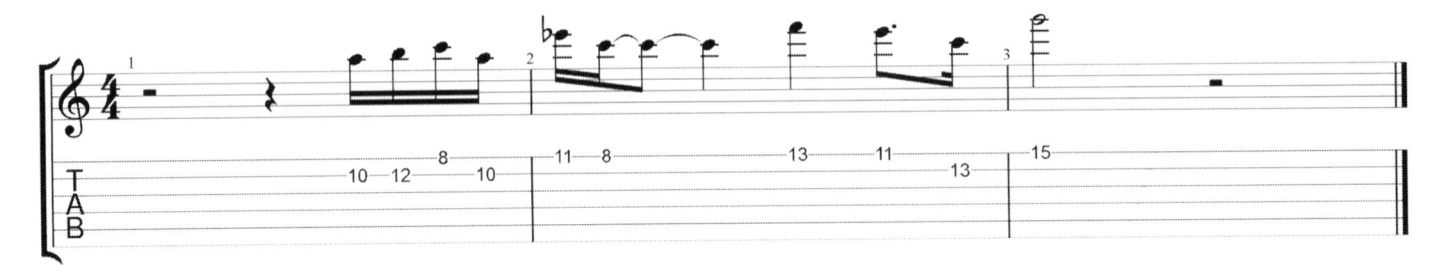

Example 6 | Track 6

This example is resolved to the 3rd.

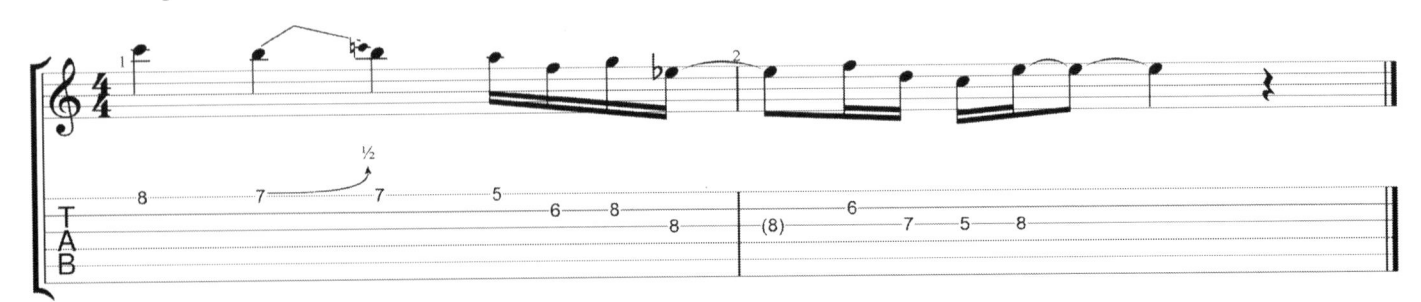

Below are some examples of the major 7th 'sweet note':

Example 7 | Track 7

This is resolved to the 3rd.

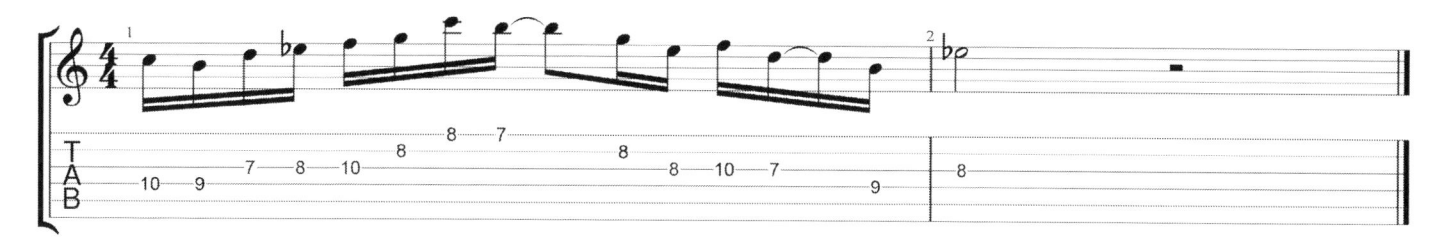

Example 8 | Track 8

Resolved to the 3rd.

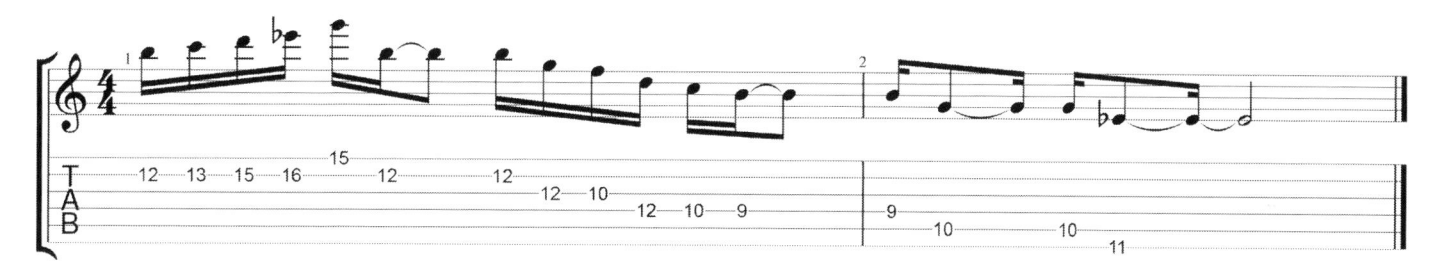

Example 9 | Track 9

This is resolved to the 3rd.

When playing your own lines it's always a good idea to finish phrases on notes other than the root of the chord. As a starting point, we recommend targeting the home notes as they outline the fundamental qualities of the chord. You should experiment with finishing on every note in the scale and work out which ones sound best to you.

Apply It To Your Style

Now that you are becoming familiar with the Melodic Minor mode and how to balance its 'sweet notes', let's have a look at the mode when played over the rock backing-track, provided on the free audio download.

As mentioned at the beginning of this chapter, a popular place to use the Melodic Minor mode is over minor7 chords. In this case, is implied by the C5 chord. In this instance we will only use the Melodic Minor mode over one chord in each example, the rest will be using standard pentatonic scales. This will give you an idea of how Melodic Minor will sound through a common chord progression.

Next are some examples of the C Melodic Minor mode that can be played over the standard rock backing track:

Example 10 | Track 10

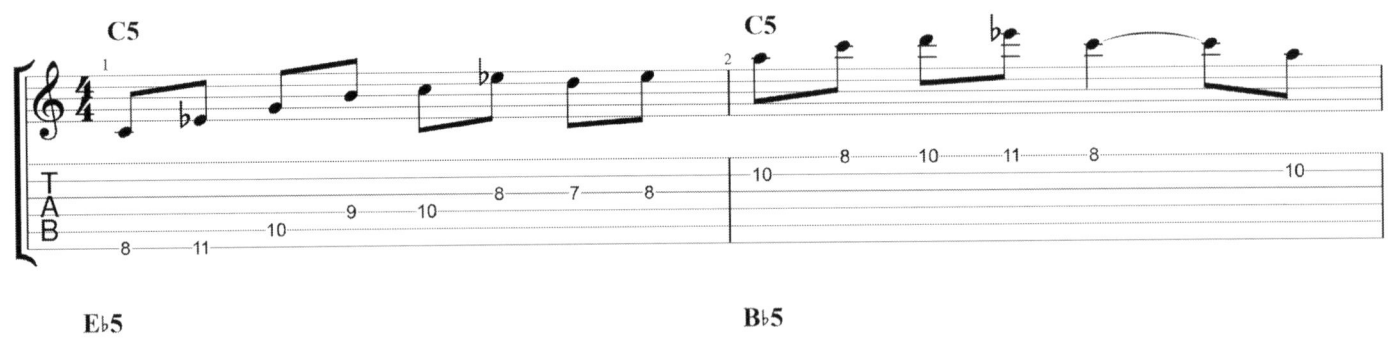

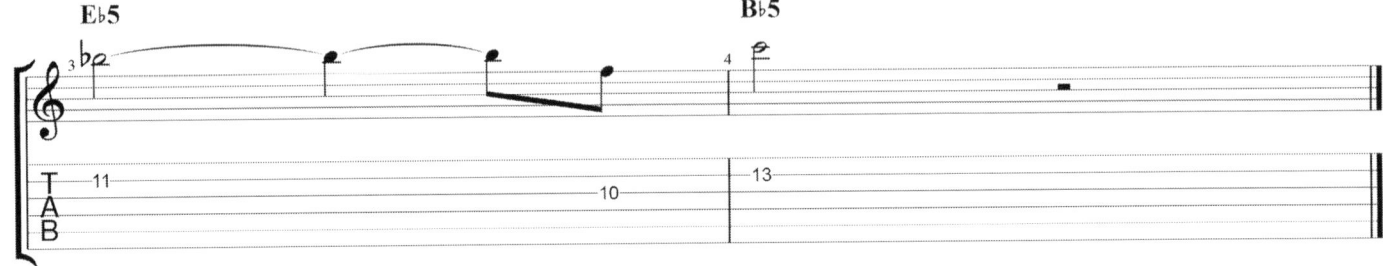

Example 11 | Track 11

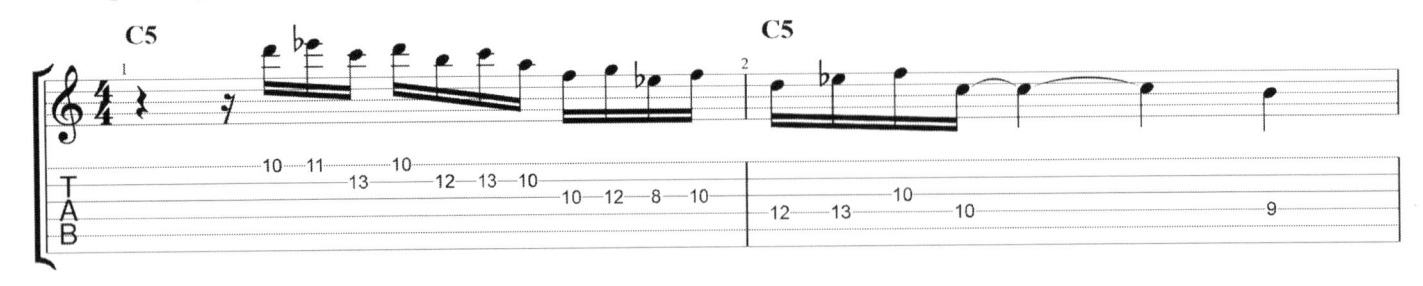

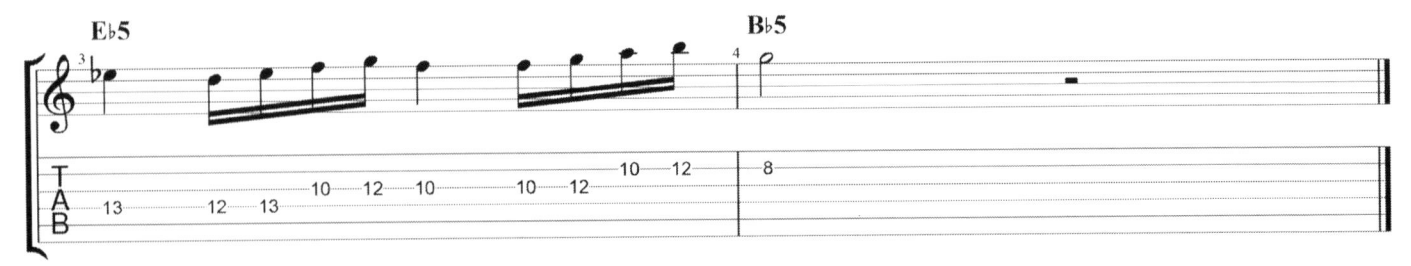

Example 12 | Track 12

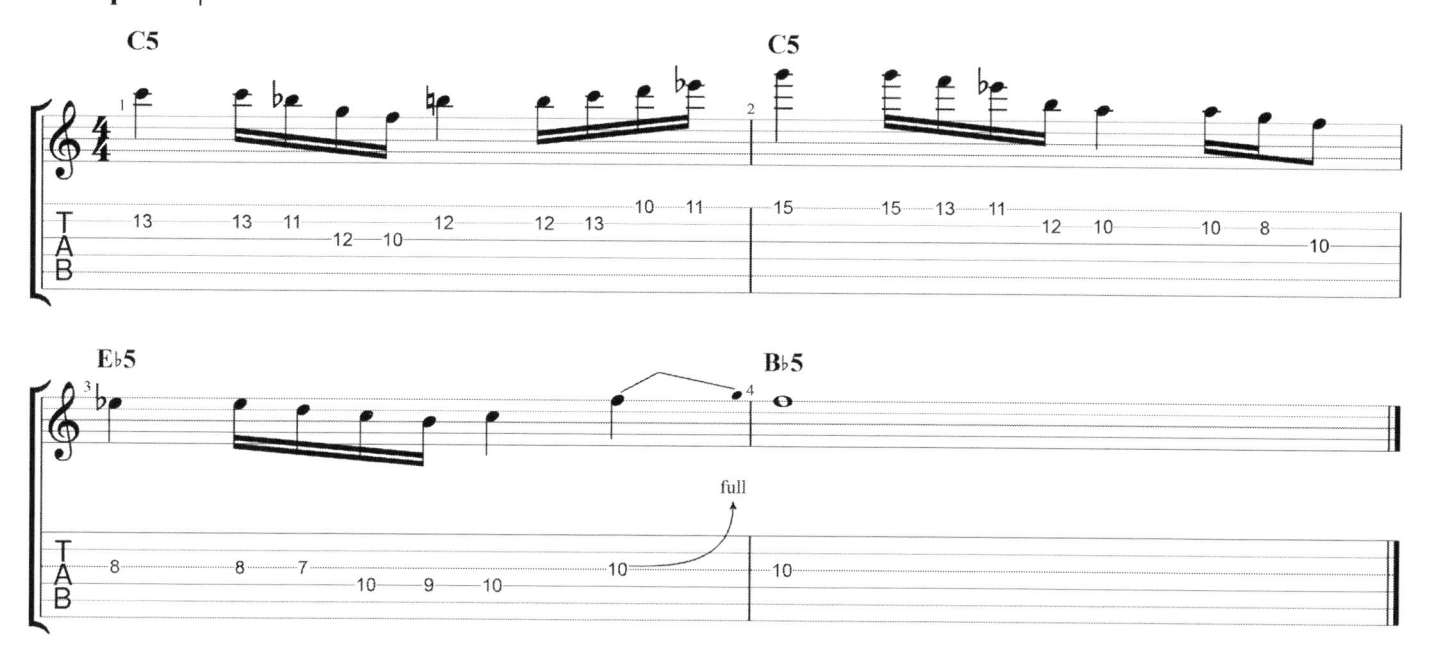

Example 13 | Track 13

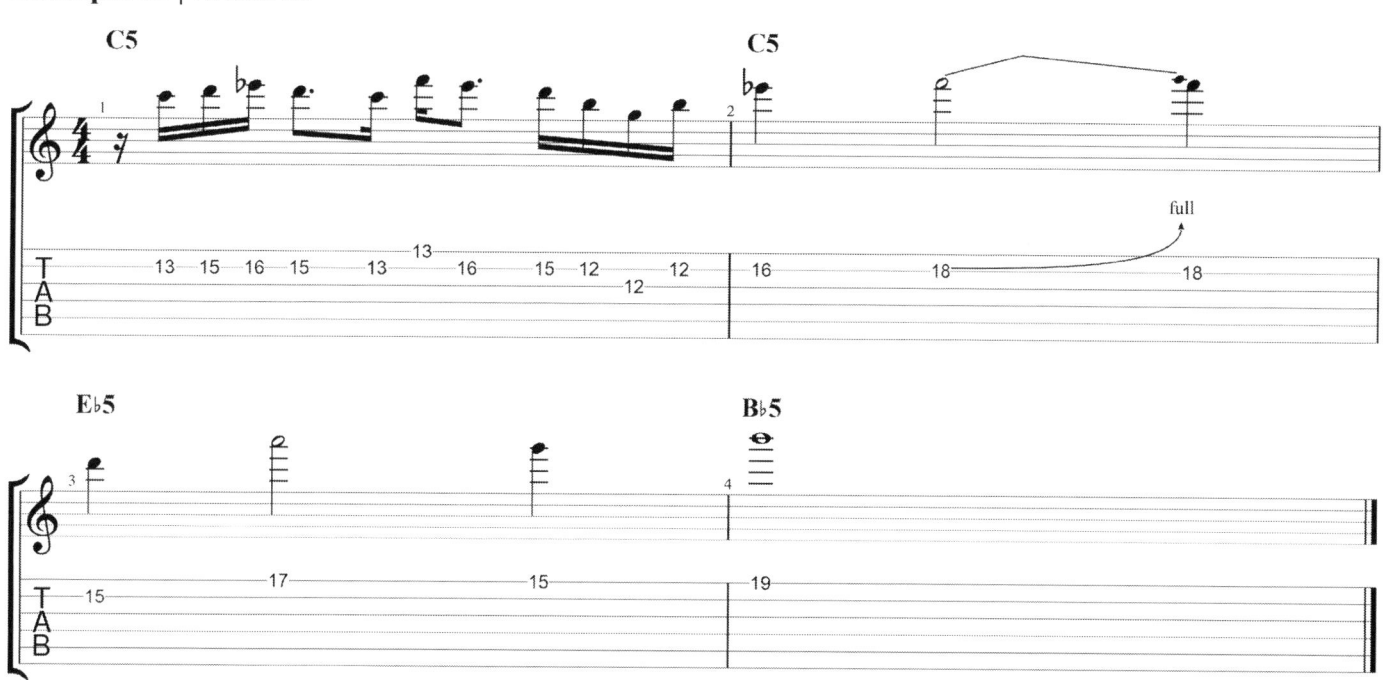

Practice these licks over the backing tracks provided on the audio download. Remember that you are not restricted to playing up and down the mode; experiment with different intervals and resolutions. Take what you've learned and apply it to your practice routine. Remember, you are just trying to add flavour to what you already know.

D Dorian b2

2nd Mode of C Melodic Minor

The Dorian b2 mode is as the name suggests a Dorian mode with a flattened second degree. However, it can be difficult to use, this is primarily due to the presence of both b2nd and major 6th intervals. Still, with some care and a bit of practice the Dorian b2 mode can be turned into an effective asset in any guitarist's arsenal.

Mode Positions

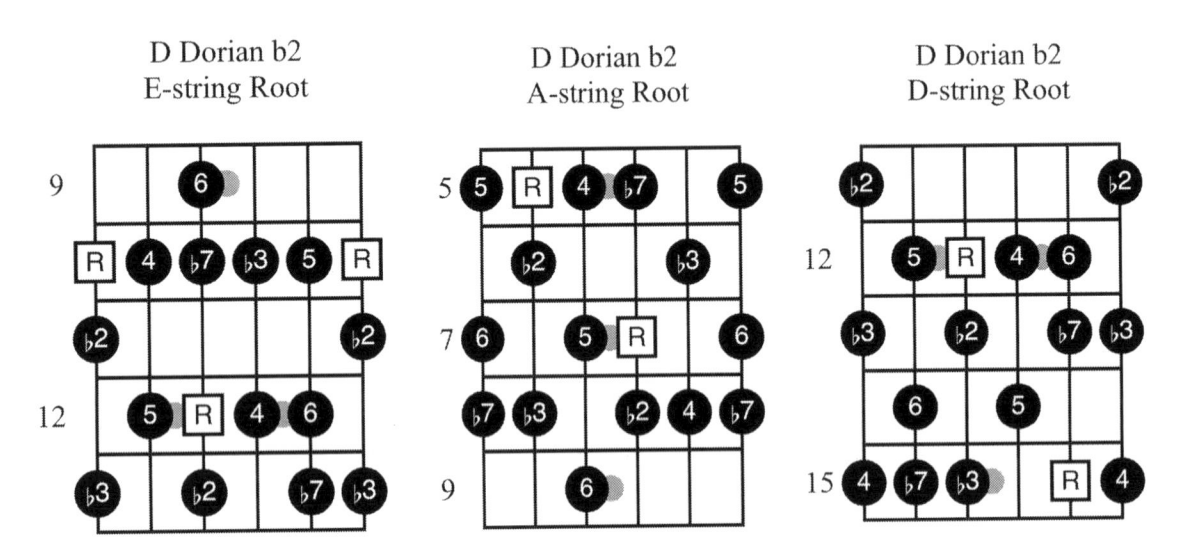

D Dorian b2 — E-string Root

D Dorian b2 — A-string Root

D Dorian b2 — D-string Root

Practice these patterns to familiarise yourself with this mode. Play the mode over the minor7 and minor7b9 chords.

Chord Diagrams

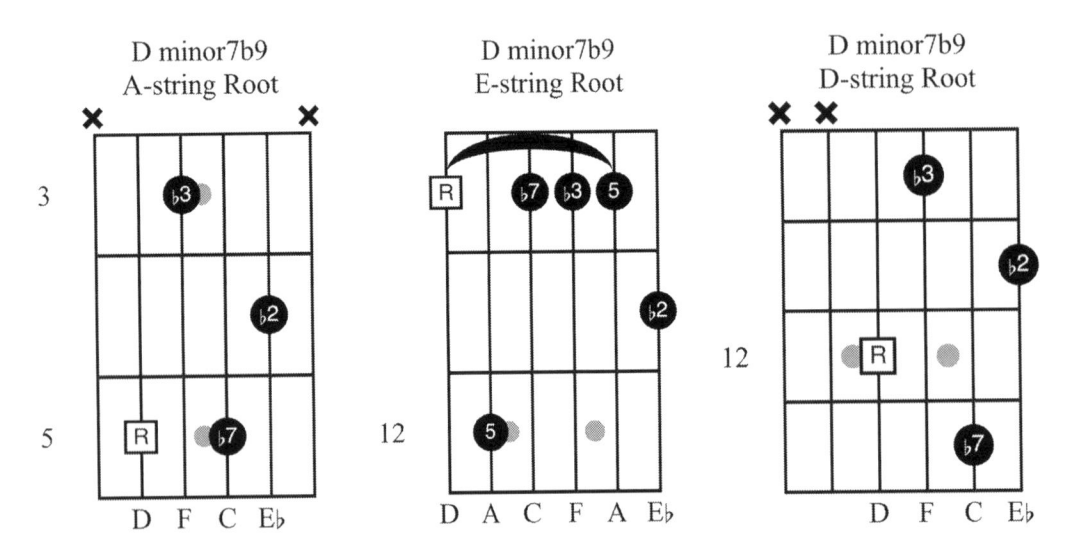

D minor7b9 — A-string Root

D minor7b9 — E-string Root

D minor7b9 — D-string Root

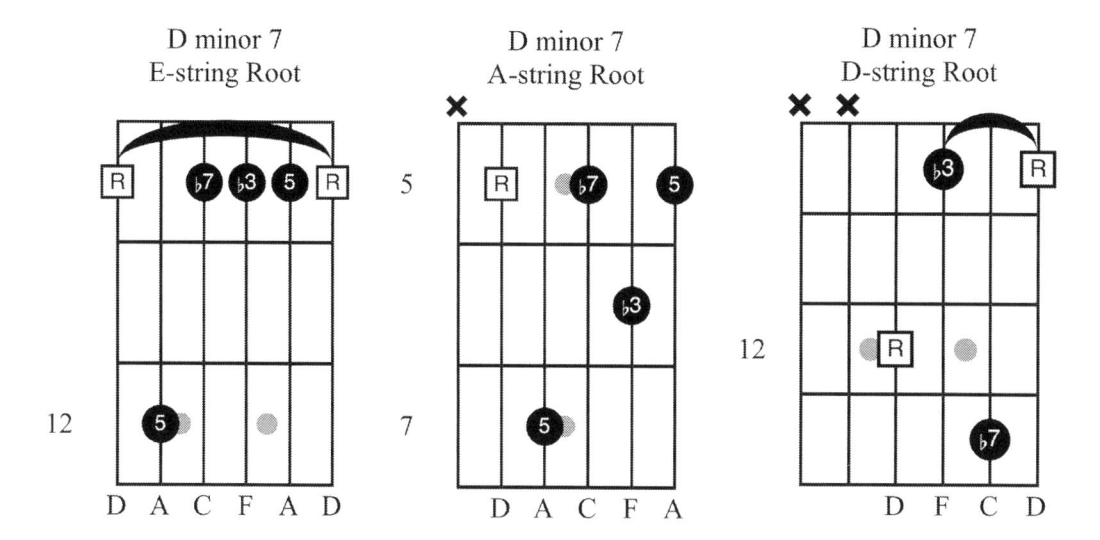

                D minor 7   D minor 7   D minor 7
              E-string Root   A-string Root   D-string Root

Even though this mode contains a b2, it can still be used over minor7 chords because the mode and the chord have a minor 3rd and minor 7th in common. The b2 adds a darker flavour. This is clearly outlined in our arpeggios

You may come across different names for all of the Melodic Minor modes. Some of these may be incorrect. We find the best way to avoid any confusion is to learn the modes as a shape. E.g. The Dorian b2 mode can also be thought of as Phrygian natural 6, and both these names are technically correct. The names we have used in this book are some of the more common titles.

Cooking with Arpeggios

The next step in order to become familiar with the sound of the Dorian b2 mode is to play the arpeggio.

These are some D Dorian b2 arpeggios:

Example 1 | Track 14

What we have here is a minor7 arpeggio. While we can indeed derive this arpeggio from the Dorian b2 mode, and use it to play over minor7 chords, it doesn't really deliver the modes distinct flavour.

D minor 7
arpeggio - Root position

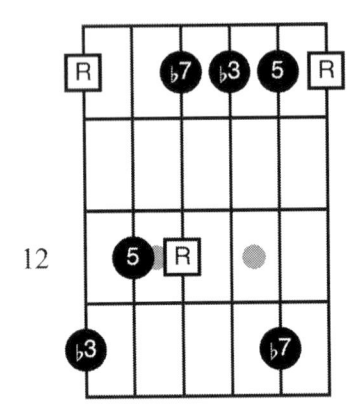

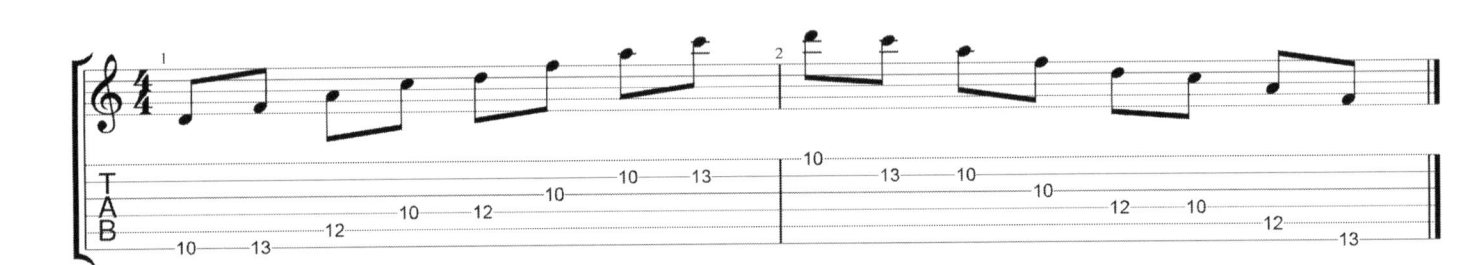

To spice this arpeggio up we're going to add a couple of 'sweet notes' to our mixture. We're going to use the b2nd and the major 6th intervals to establish the Dorian b2 sound.

This is the Dorian b2 arpeggio that focuses on the b2nd and major 6th intervals:

Example 2 | Track 15

Here is a D Dorian b2 arpeggio in root position. Notice how this arpeggio has more of a distinct character than the minor7 arpeggio. Try to pay attention to how this scale sounds over a D minor7 chord, with our 'sweet notes' adding tension to the chord.

D Dorian b2
arpeggio - Root Position

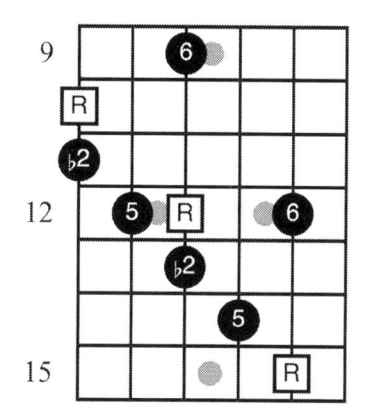

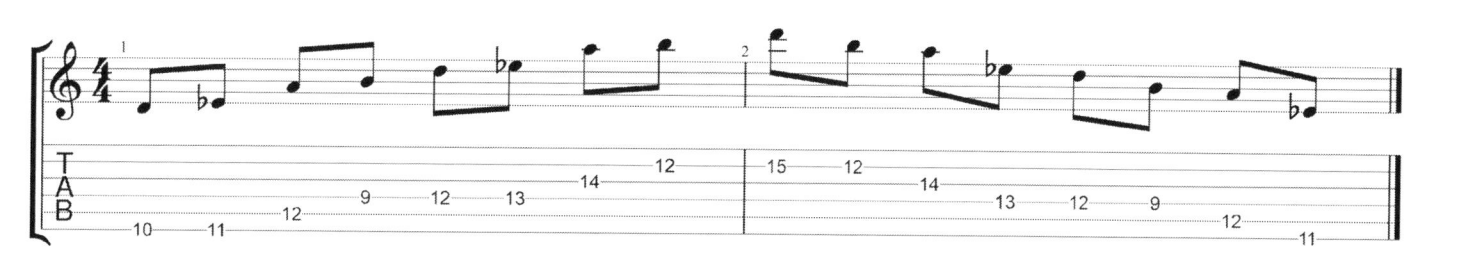

Example 3 | Track 16

D Dorian b2 arpeggio in 1st inversion. Pay attention to the stretch at the end of this arpeggio. Experiment with slides, hammer-ons and pull-offs to achieve a fluid motion.

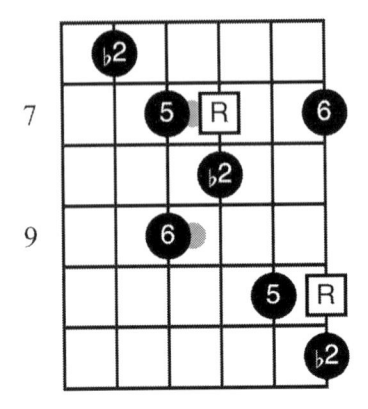

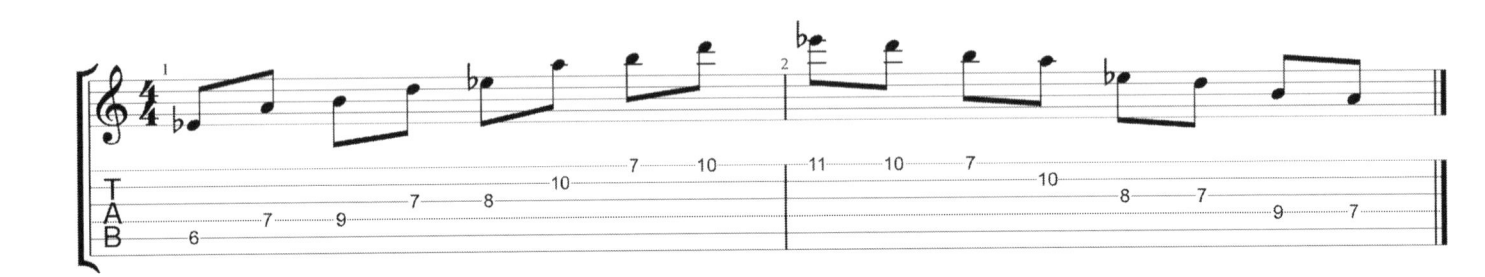

Example 4 | Track 17

D Dorian b2 arpeggio in 2nd inversion. Play in either octave. We suggest playing it high as playing it low can sound muddy against the chord.

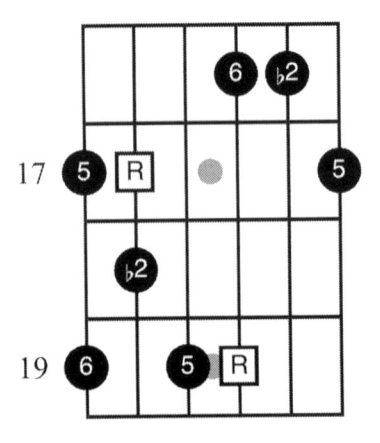

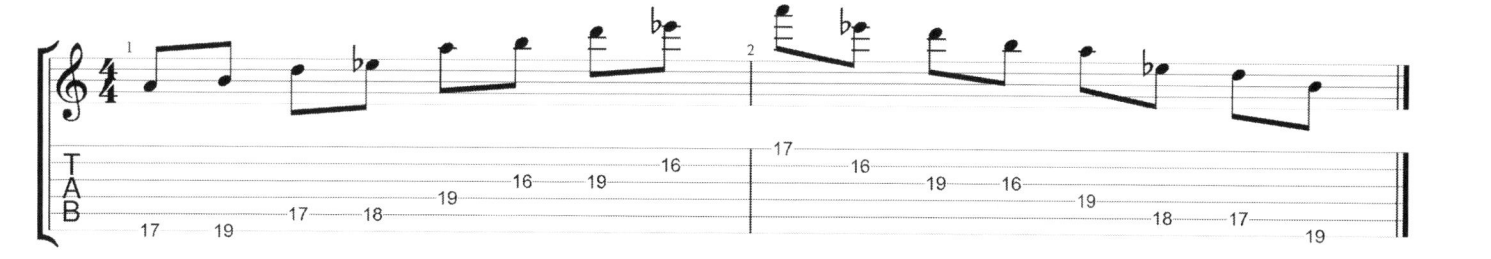

Practice these patterns over the backing track provided at the end of each example on the free audio download. Use these arpeggios as starting points for writing your own solos.

Targeting The Sweet Notes

As we mentioned before, the 'sweet notes' of the Dorian b2 mode are the b2nd and major 6th intervals. By basing licks around these two notes we can clearly hear the tonal qualities of the Dorian b2 mode, but these notes must be handled with care.

Food For Thought

The b2nd interval in the Dorian b2 mode is an outside note. Outside notes are an effective way to spice up your playing with tension and release. It is best to avoid lingering on these notes for too long as you can lose your connection to the key centre.

The key to effectively using these 'sweet notes' is in how you resolve them. We find that both the b2nd and major 6th intervals can resolve easily to the 5th; in this case an A. Resolving the b2nd to the 5th outlines an augmented 4th interval, which creates a sense of tension and release. Whereas resolving the major 6th interval to the 5th is purely practical due to how close they are.

Below are some examples based around the b2nd 'sweet note':

Example 5 | Track 18

Here we are resolving to the root. In this example, be sure to give the tied note values their proper length.

Example 6 | Track 19

This is resolving to the 5th. Take care with the half bend, make sure to not under bend the note.

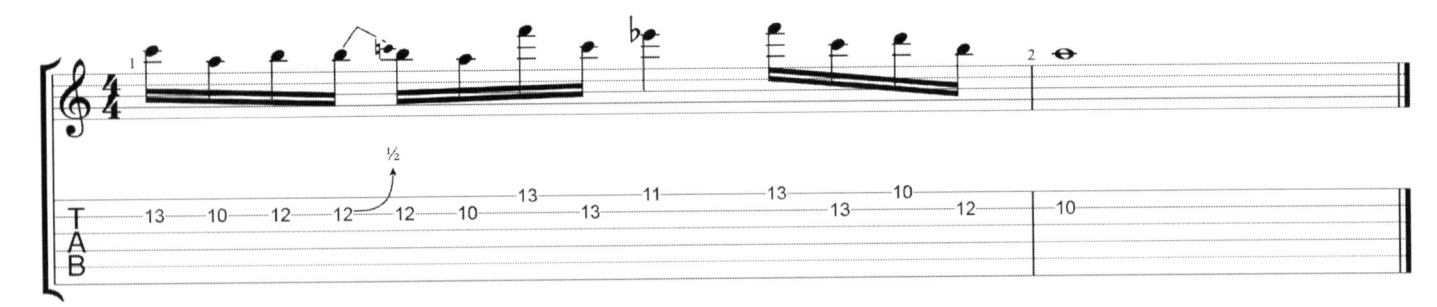

Example 7 | Track 20

Here, we are resolving to the minor 3rd. Focus on playing these 16th notes fluently

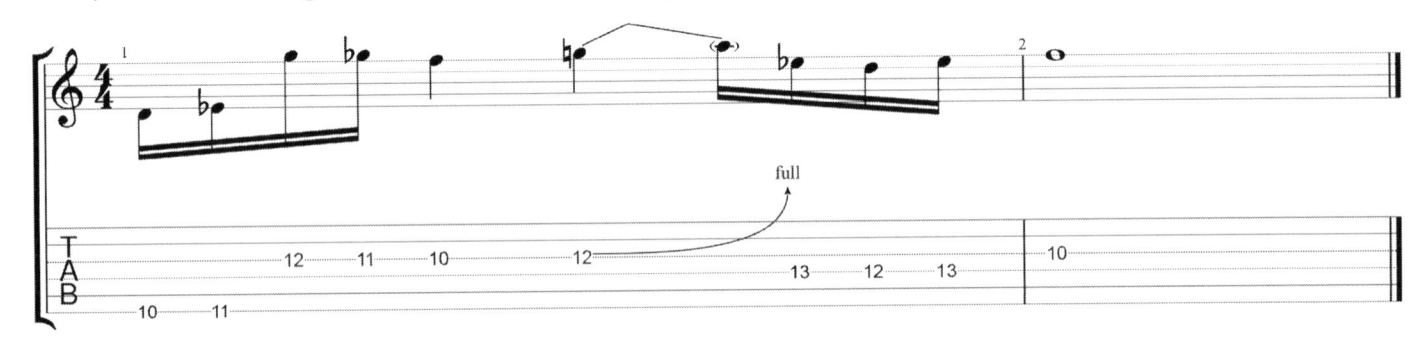

Next are some examples of the major 6th 'sweet note':

Example 8 | Track 21

This line resolves to the 3rd.

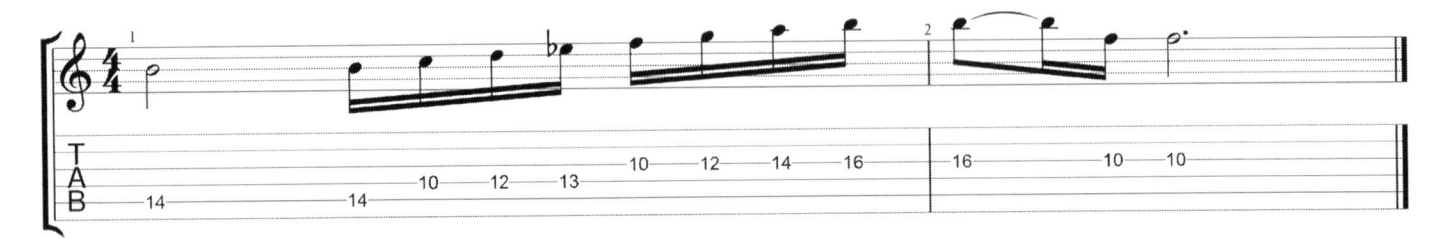

Example 9 | Track 22

Here we are resolving to the 2nd. Take care with the full bend, make sure to not under bend the note.

```
e|--------------------------------------------------|
B|--------------------------------------------------|
G|--17--17--15--19-----------------15---------------|
D|--------------18---------17-----------18--16--(16)|
A|--------------------------------------------------|
E|--------------------------------------------------|
       full
```

Example 10 | Track 23

Here we are resolving to the 6th. Dotted notes can be tricky to play. It's easier if you count the rhythm out before playing the lick.

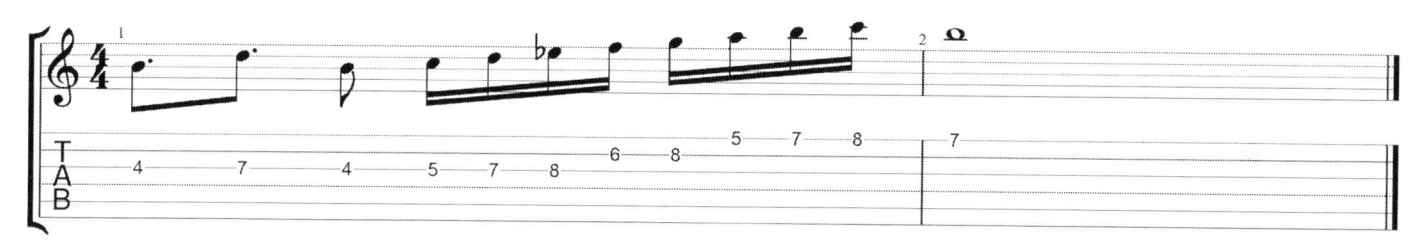

```
e|-----------------------------------5--7--8--7-----|
B|---------------------------6--8-------------------|
G|--4-----7-----4-----5--7--8-----------------------|
D|--------------------------------------------------|
A|--------------------------------------------------|
E|--------------------------------------------------|
```

In these examples, we can see that the 'sweet notes' are being used as passing notes. Practice utilising these 'sweet notes' in your own playing so you can further understand how these 'sweet notes' work.

Apply It To Your Style

Now that you're starting to grasp the Dorian b2 mode, it's time to integrate it into your playing. Remember that this mode can be used over standard minor7 chords as well as minor7b9 chords.

Beneath are some examples of the D Dorian b2 mode to be played over the standard rock backing track:

Example 11 | Track 24

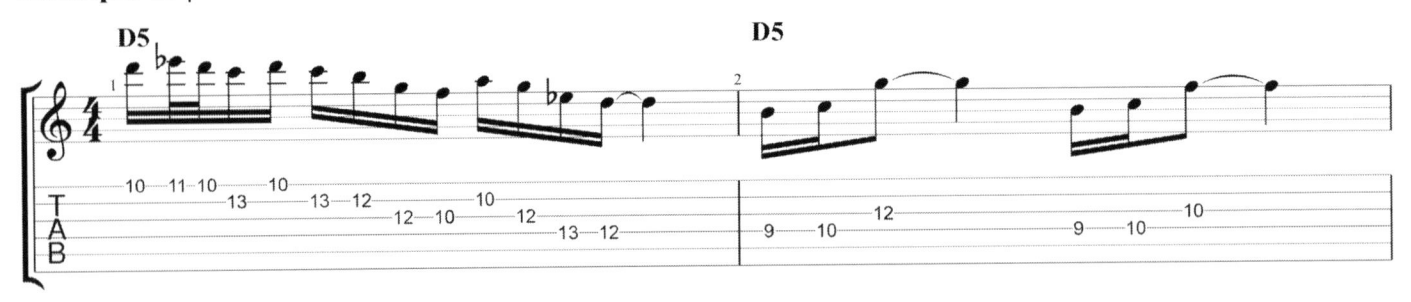

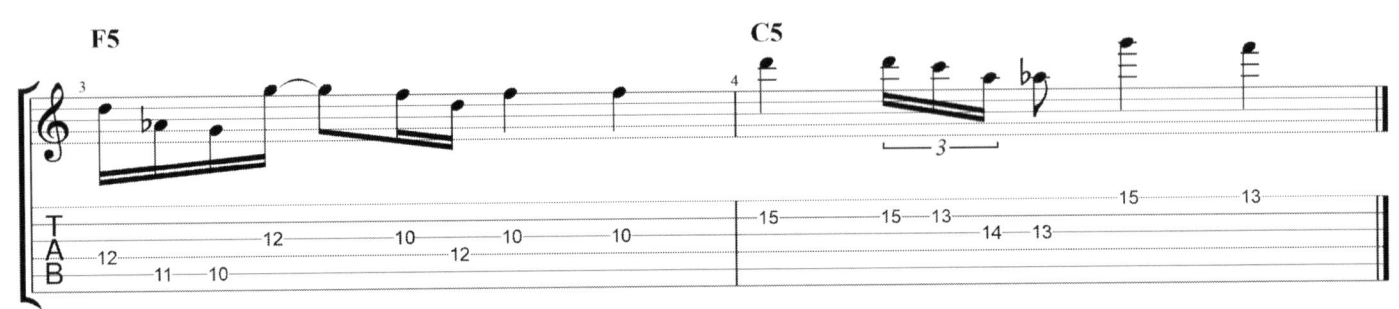

Example 12 | Track 25

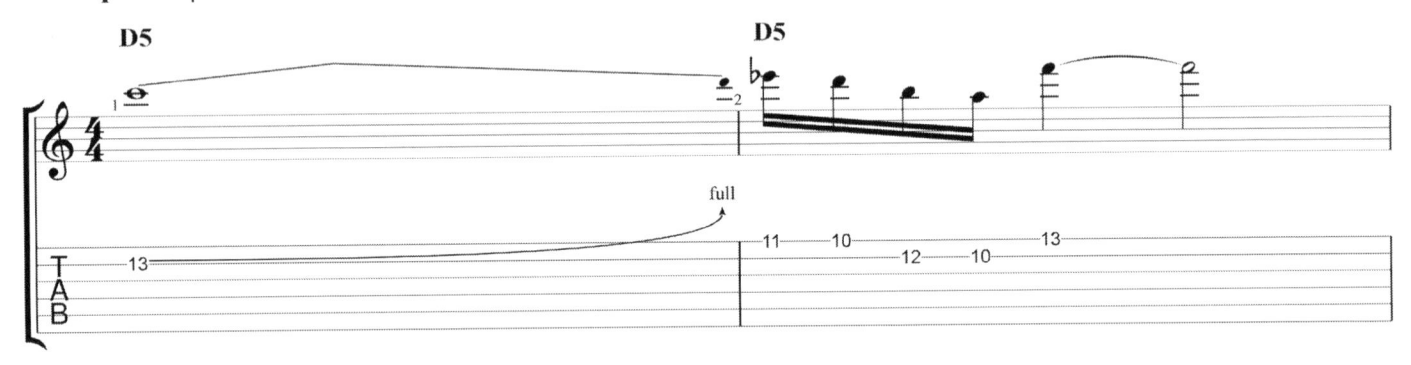

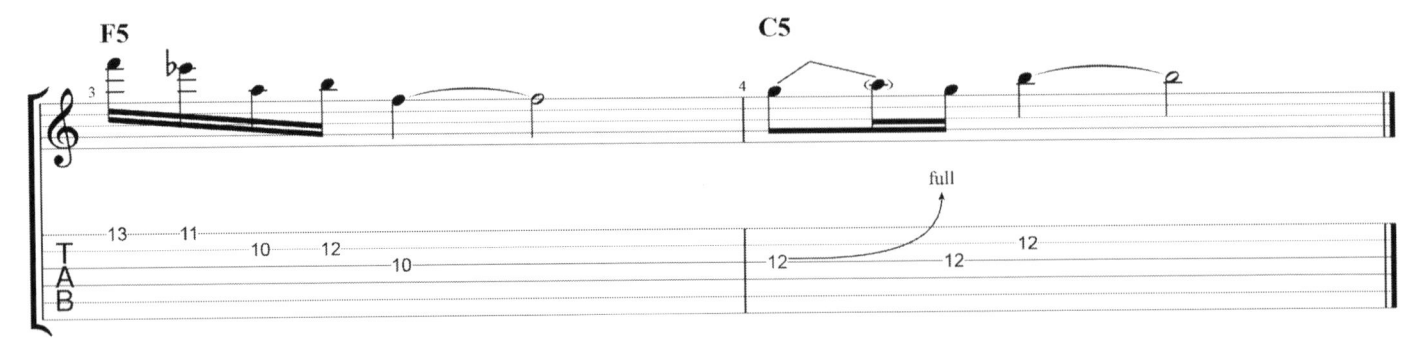

Example 13 | Track 26

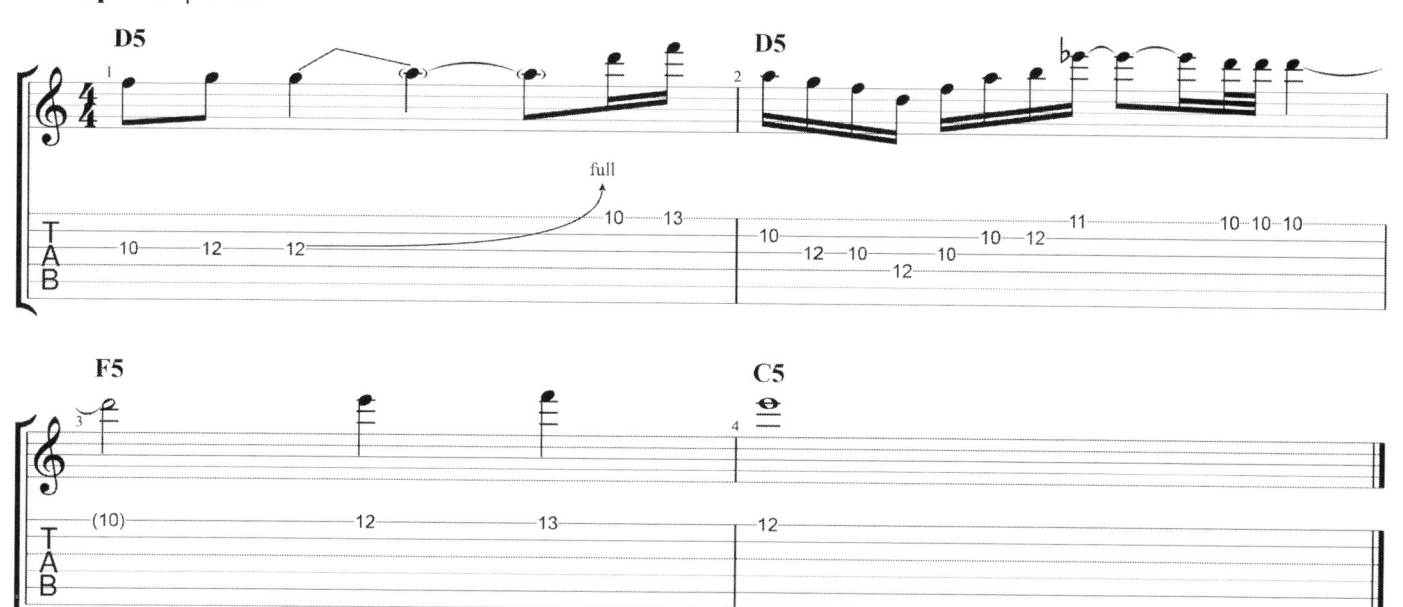

Example 14 | Track 27

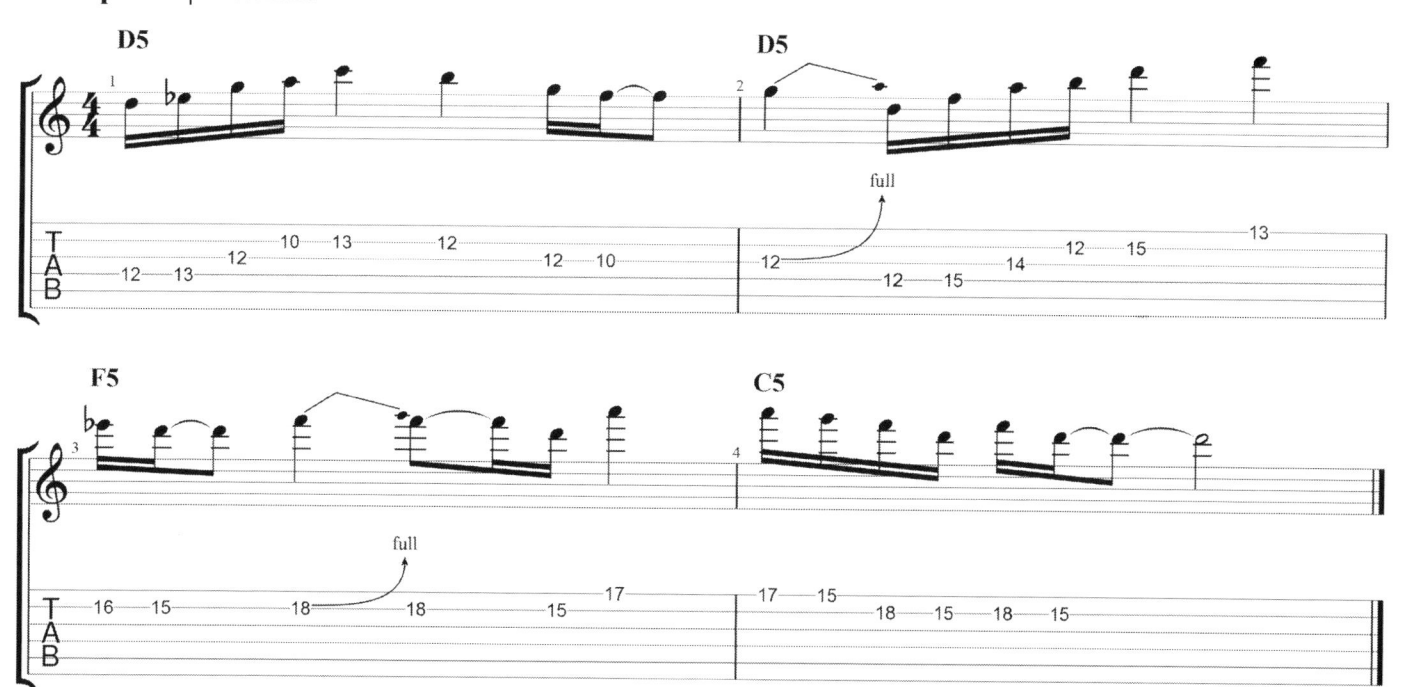

Take what you've learnt in this chapter and apply it to your practice routine. You can practice your ideas over the backing tracks provided at the end of each example. Get creative with the mode, don't restrict yourself to just playing up and down each scale. Start out slowly and build to what you already know.

Eb Lydian #5

3rd Mode of C Melodic Minor

Next up is the Lydian #5 mode which is the third mode of Melodic Minor. This mode is the Lydian mode with an augmented fifth degree. Despite the awkward sound of the augmented fifth, this mode isn't as daunting as it may look.

Mode Positions

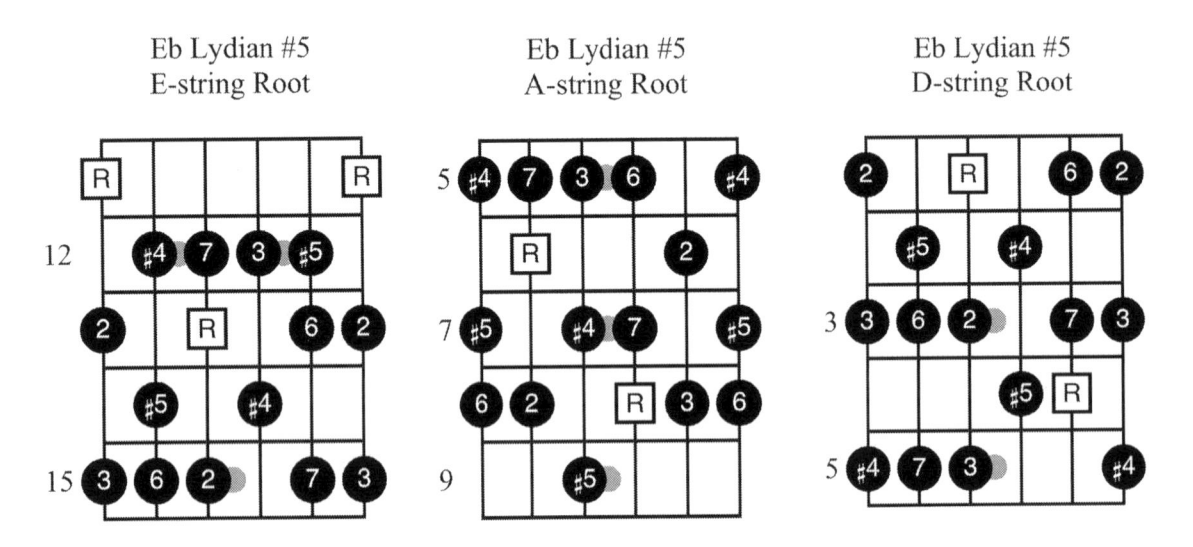

Practice these patterns to familiarise yourself with this mode. Play the mode over the major7#5 and major7 chords.

Chord Diagrams

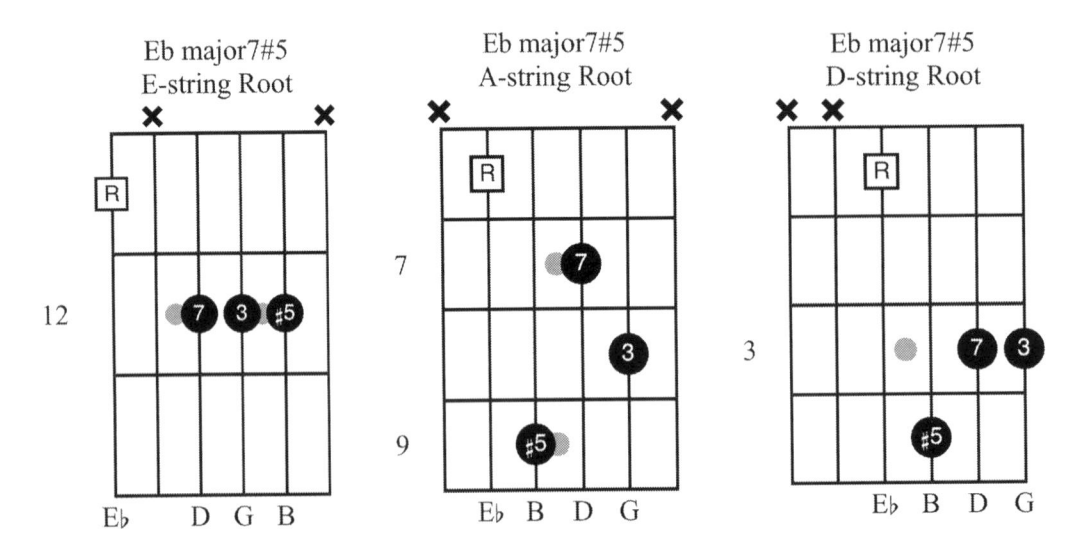

Eb major 7
E-string Root

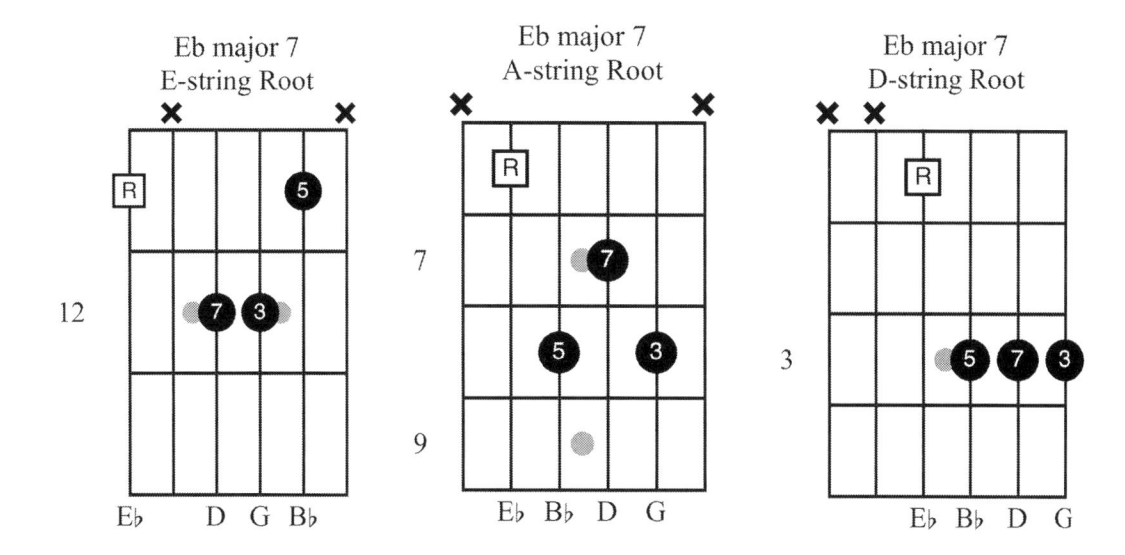

Eb major 7
A-string Root

Eb major 7
D-string Root

This mode is normally associated with major7#5 chords, however it can be equally effective when played over standard major7 chords. Remember, we have to resolve the #5 carefully because it is an outside note that can cause dissonance

Food For Thought

When you come across an augmented interval, it means the note has been raised by a semitone. E.g. an augmented 5th interval is the same as a #5 interval.

Cooking With Arpeggios

The next thing to do in order to become familiar with the sound of the Lydian #5 mode is to play the arpeggio.

Below are some Eb Lydian #5 arpeggios:

Example 1 | Track 28

This shows an Eb Lydian #5 arpeggio in root position. The first three notes of this arpeggio, Eb, G and B, form an augmented triad. This is the defining feature of this mode as it outlines the only point of difference between this and the regular Lydian scale.

Eb Lydian #5
arpeggio - Root position

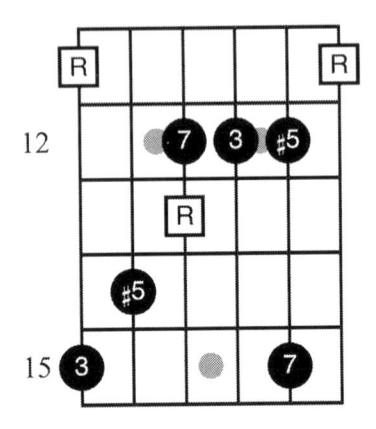

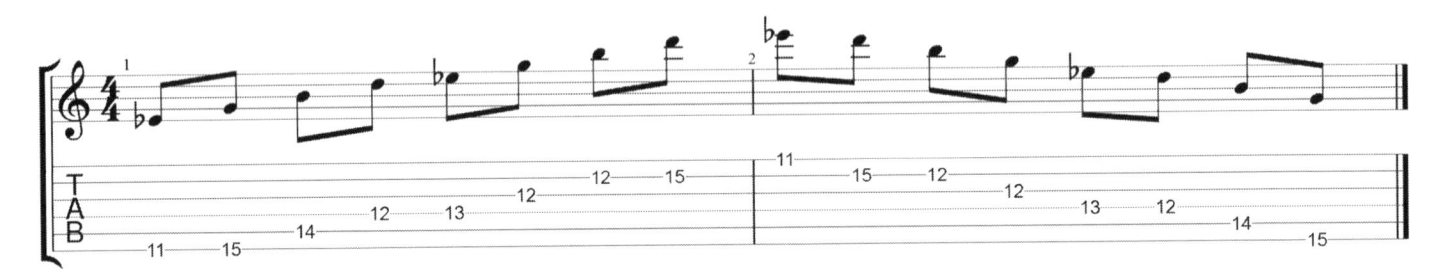

Example 2 | Track 29

Eb Lydian #5 arpeggio in 1st inversion. Be aware of the stretches in this arpeggio, try hammer-ons and pull-offs to get a smooth sound.

Eb Lydian #5
arpeggio - 1st Inversion

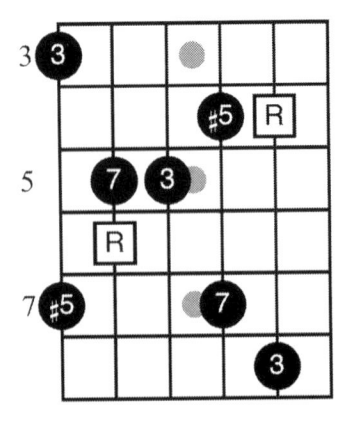

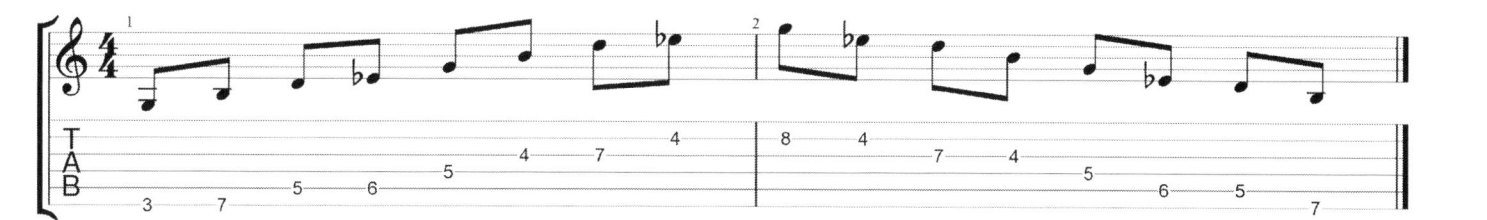

Example 3 | Track 30

What we have here is an Eb Lydian #5 arpeggio launched from the #5. Start out slow in this one, it can get crowded in the higher end of this arpeggio.

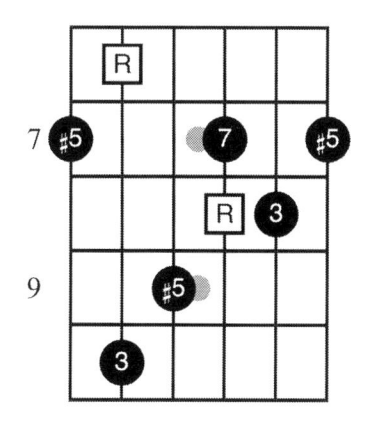

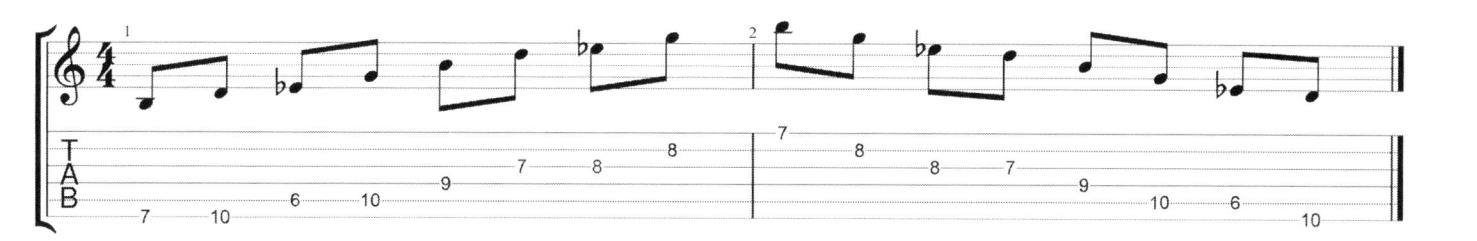

Eb Lydian #5
arpeggio - 2nd Inversion

The presence of this augmented triad* is something of a double-edged sword as it creates dissonance in what, is otherwise, a pleasant sounding mode. The key to dealing with this dissonance is knowing how to resolve the #5 correctly.

Practice these patterns over the backing track provided at the end of each example on the free audio download. Use these arpeggios as starting points for writing your own solos.

*An augmented triad is a triad where all the notes are a major 3rd apart.

Targeting The Sweet Notes

We consider the #5 to be the only 'sweet note' of this mode as it is the only note that separates it from the Lydian mode. This note gives the Lydian #5 mode its individual identity.

If we were playing over a Eb major7 chord, it would be easy to land on the #5 and create the Lydian #5 sound; however, this would not be an effective use of this mode as dissonance is only half of the effect – in order to be fully effective, dissonance must be resolved. It is possible to resolve the #5 to the major 3rd, but you could also resolve it to the major 6th; it comes down to personal taste. Try your own combinations and decide what appeals to you.

Next are some examples based around the #5 'sweet note':

Example 4 | Track 31

In this example we can hear how the dissonance of the #5 disrupts the flow; however, we can also see that this disruption is easily dealt with by resolving to the major 3rd.

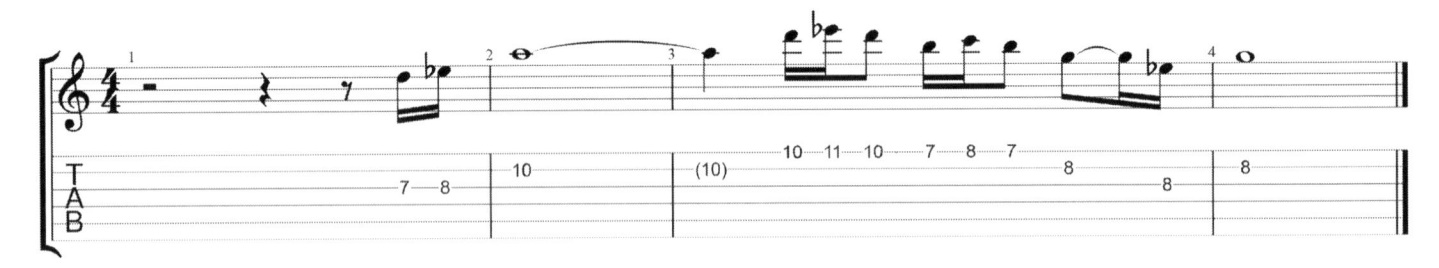

Example 5 | Track 32

Here we are resolving to the 7th.

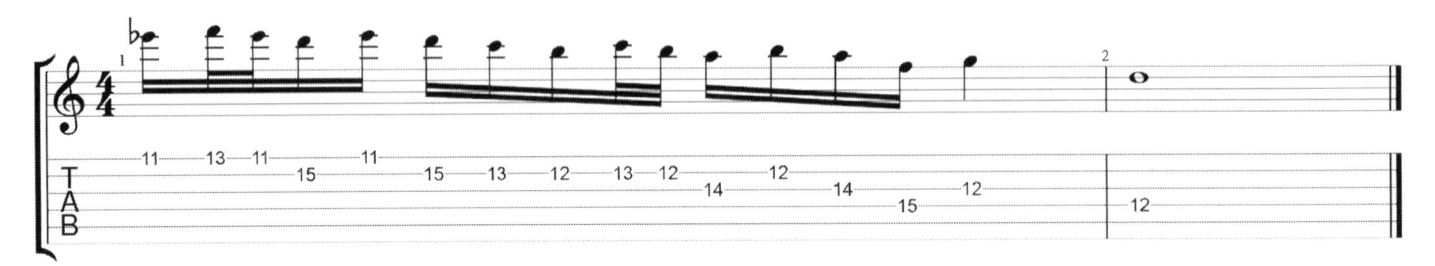

Example 6 | Track 33

This is resolving to the 6th.

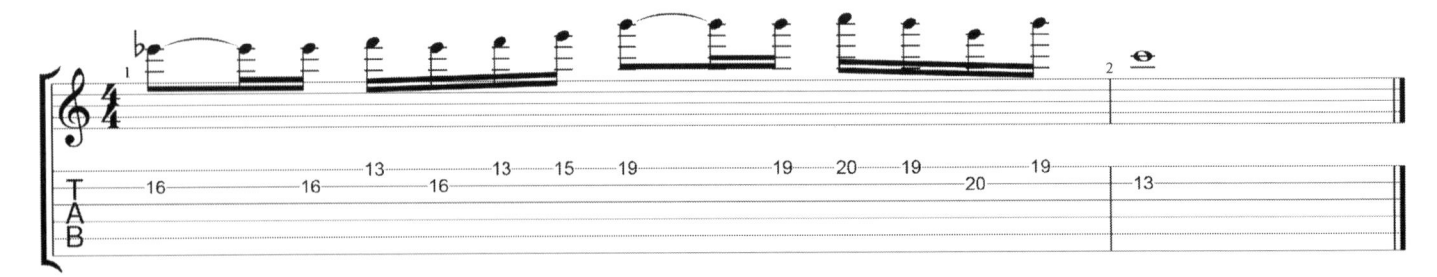

The #5 interval provides enough dissonance to create interesting lines but is most effective when used sparingly, and fortunately for us there are a lot of notes in the scale that we can resolve to.

Apply It To Your Style

Two things to remember when using this mode:

1. Subtlety – Apply the #5 sparingly.

2. Resolution – Your use of the #5 will only sound as good as your resolution of it. But don't sweat, you have lots of notes to resolve to, just experiment with them and find your favourites.

Beneath are some examples of Eb Lydian #5 to be played over the standard rock backing track:

Example 7 | Track 34

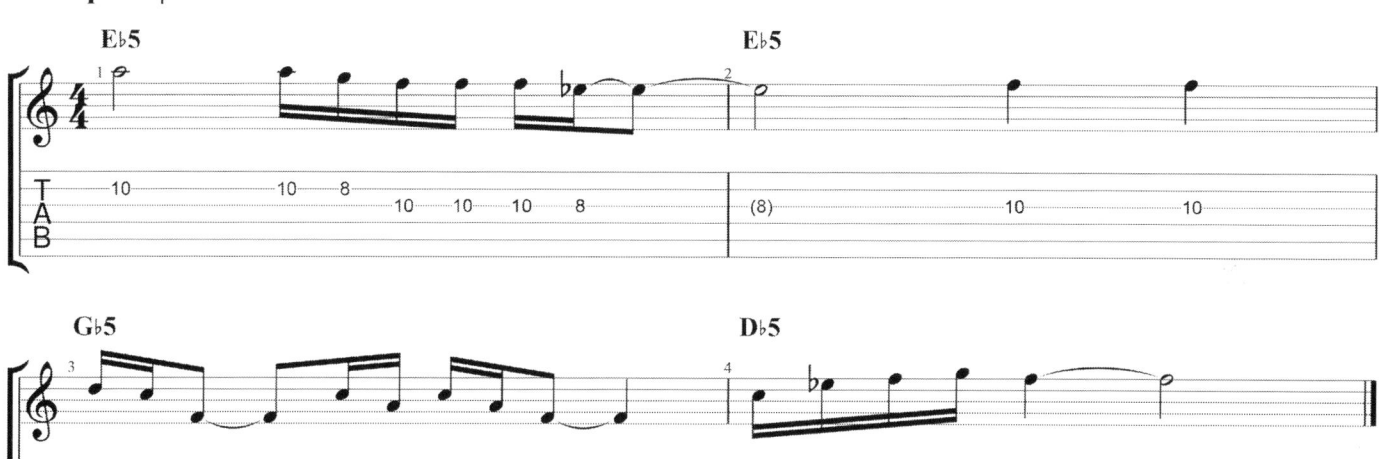

Example 8 | Track 35

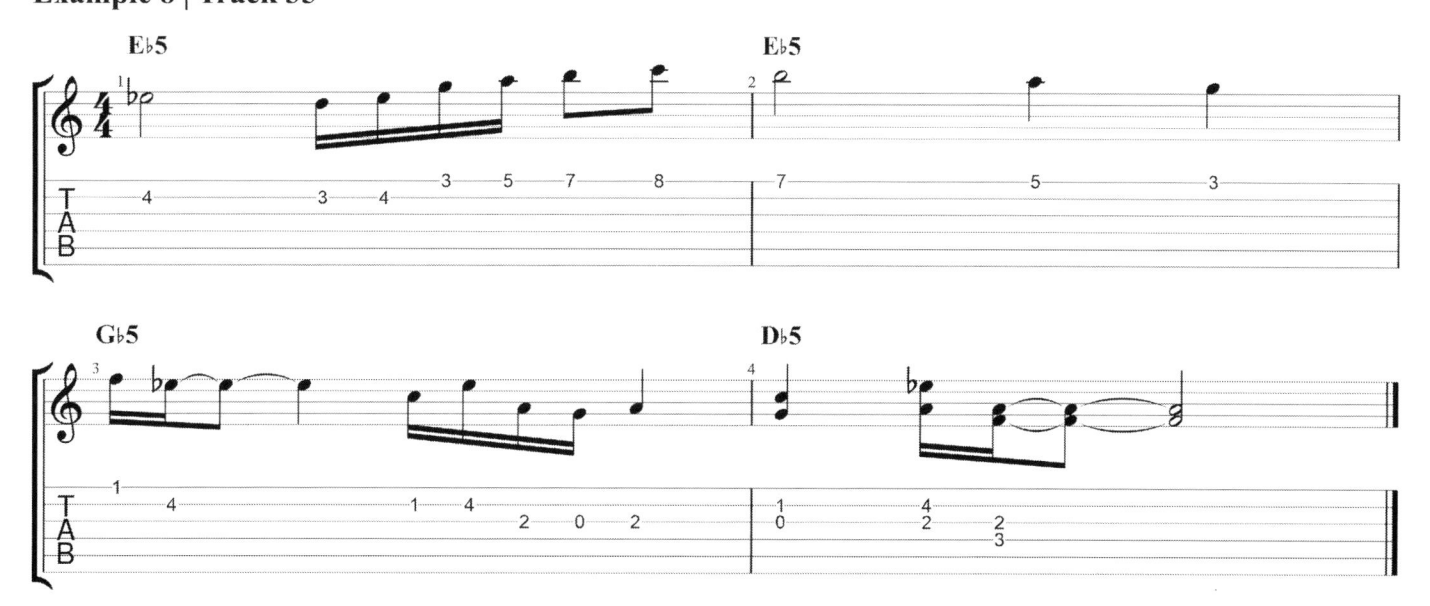

Example 9 | Track 36

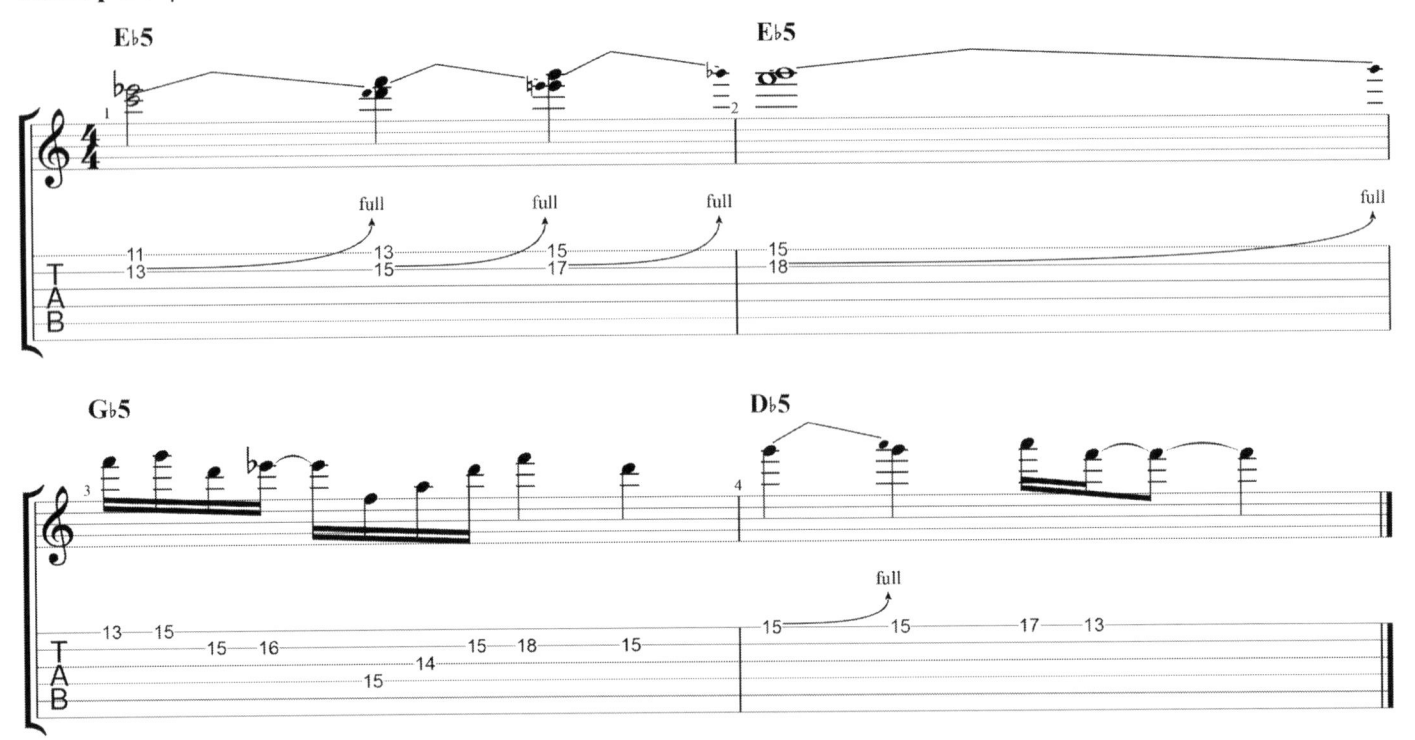

The best way to improve these modes is to incorporate them into your natural playing style. Try working a few ideas to a point where you can use them in a solo at a band practice. You will notice a massive improvement in your playing when you start taking these ideas out of the 'practice room' and into the 'real world'. Don't be disheartened if things don't start to click right away. The backing tracks provided at the end of each audio example are a great way to build some confidence into your ability.

F Lydian Dominant

4th Mode of C Melodic Minor

The Lydian Dominant mode is a great mode to bring out added flavour in V7 chords. The Lydian Dominant mode is a Mixolydian mode with a #4. Like the Mixolydian mode, it is used over V7 chords, because they share the intervallic structure of 1, 3, 5, b7. The #4 in the Lydian Dominant mode allows us to add some different tensions to V7 chords.

Mode Positions

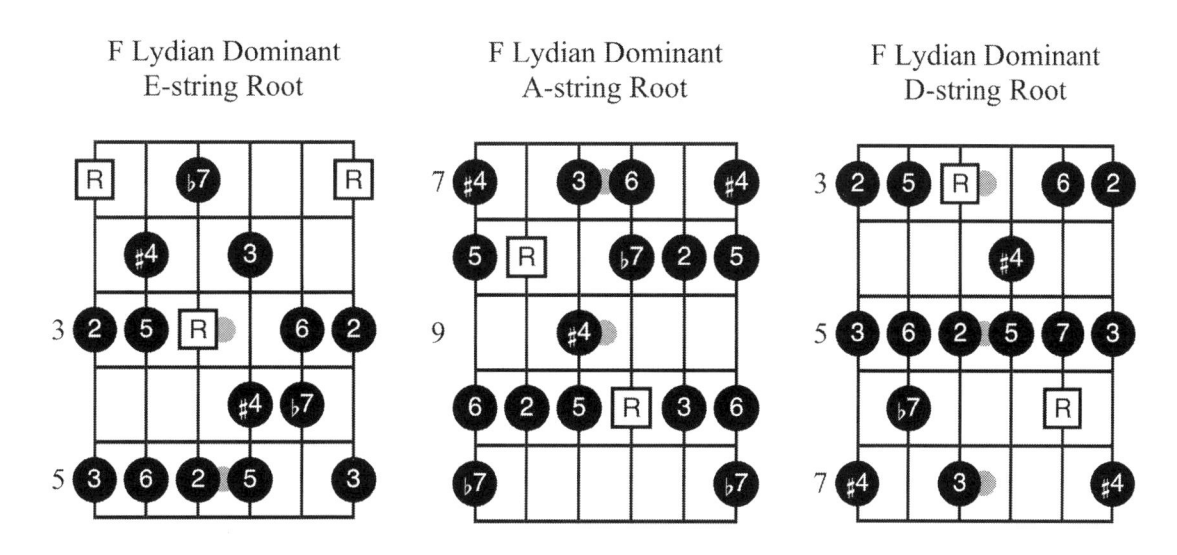

F Lydian Dominant — E-string Root

F Lydian Dominant — A-string Root

F Lydian Dominant — D-string Root

Practice these patterns to familiarise yourself with this mode. Play the mode over the V7#11 and V7 chords.

Chord Diagrams

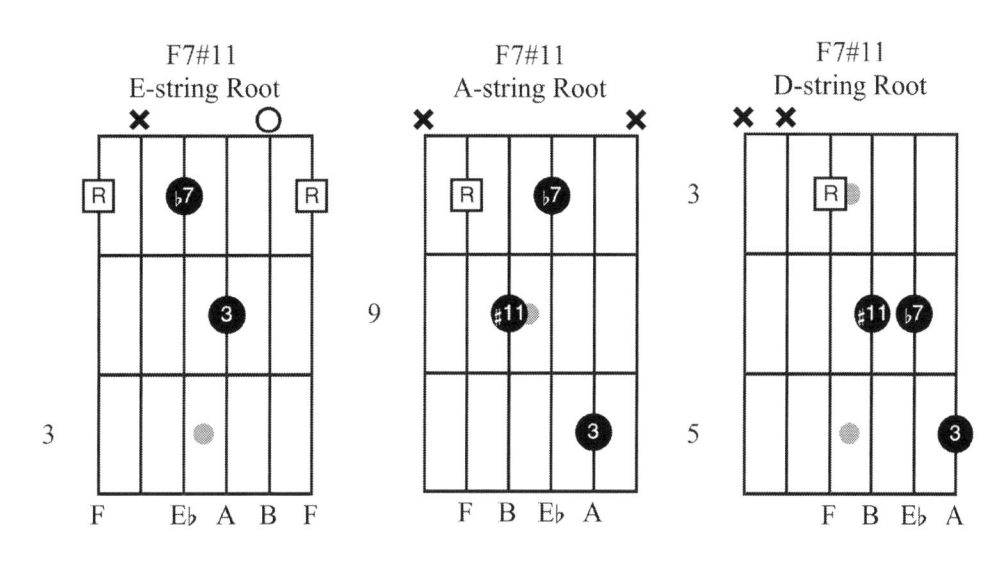

F7#11 — E-string Root
F Eb A B F

F7#11 — A-string Root
F B Eb A

F7#11 — D-string Root
F B Eb A

```
         F7                    F7                    F7
    E-string Root         A-string Root         D-string Root
```

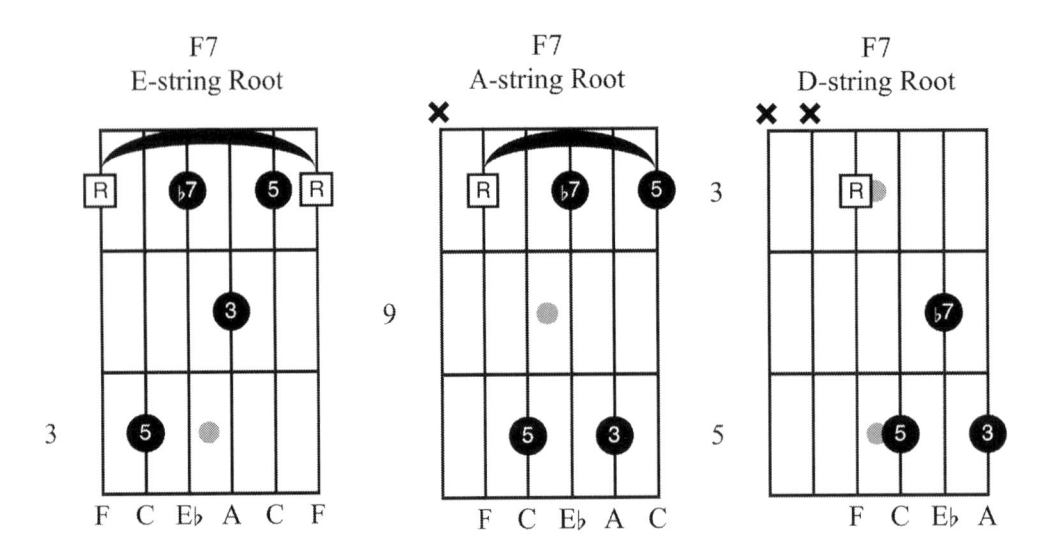

This mode is normally associated with V7#11 chords, however it can be equally effective when played over standard V7 chords. The #4 is dissonant because of how close it is to the 5th, a home note.

Cooking With Arpeggios

The next step in becoming familiar with the sound of the Lydian Dominant mode is to play the arpeggio.

These are some F Lydian Dominant arpeggios:

Example 1 | Track 37

F Lydian Dominant arpeggio in root position. Start off slow with this arpeggio as the finger position can be tricky.

F Lydian Dominant arpeggio - Root position

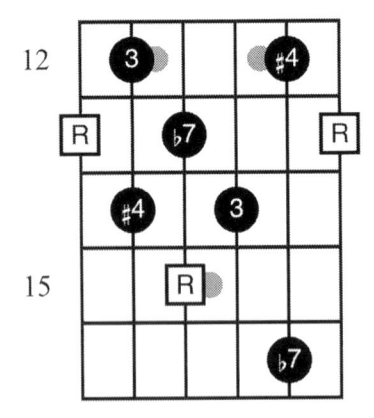

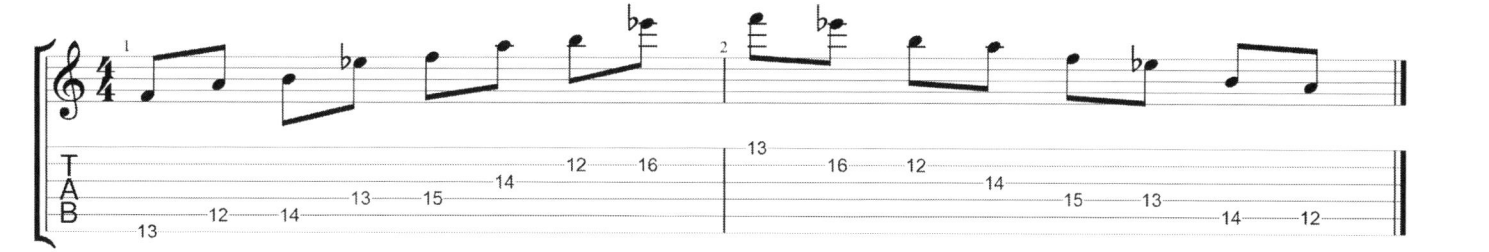

Example 2 | Track 38

F Lydian Dominant arpeggio in 1st inversion. This one is similar to example 1, but with added stretches at the end. Again, take your time to work this up.

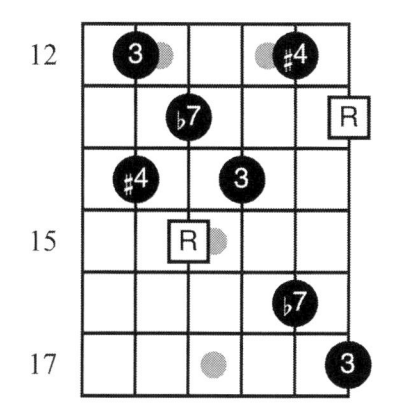

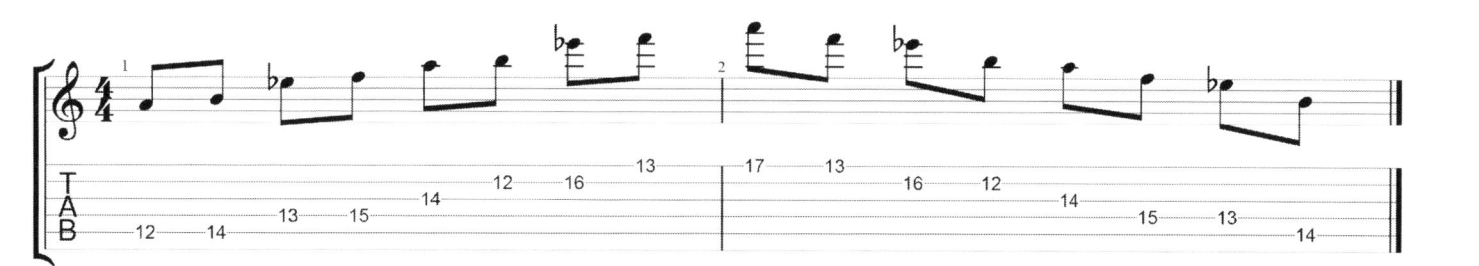

Example 3 | Track 39

F Lydian Dominant arpeggio launched off the #4. You may have noticed that this example has the same shape as example 1. The symmetry between these shapes allow us to learn the mode on other parts of the fretboard.

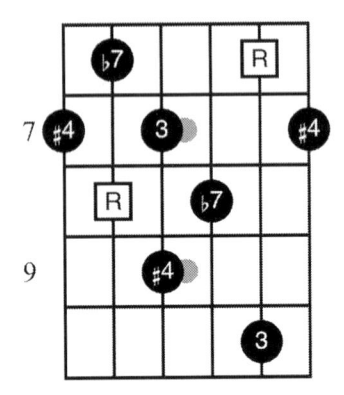

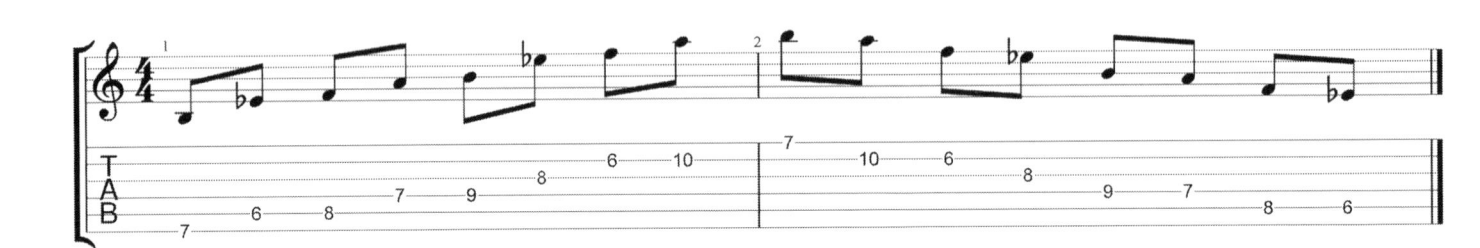

Practice these patterns over the backing track provided at the end of each example on the free audio download. Use these arpeggios as starting points for writing your own solos.

Targeting The Sweet Notes

The 'sweet notes' of the Lydian Dominant mode are the #4 and b7 intervals. In the key of F, these are B and Eb. An effective way to deal with the #4 is to resolve it down a tone to the major 3rd (A). This tension and release is moving from the augmented 4th to the resolution point of the 3rd, which is a home note. Likewise the b7 can be resolved to any home note.

Below are some examples of the #4 'sweet note':

Example 4 | Track 40

This example shows that dissonance is created between the F and B. This is resolved by playing an A. This is dropping the B down a tone thus changing the interval from an augmented 4th to a major 3rd, which is a lot more pleasant.

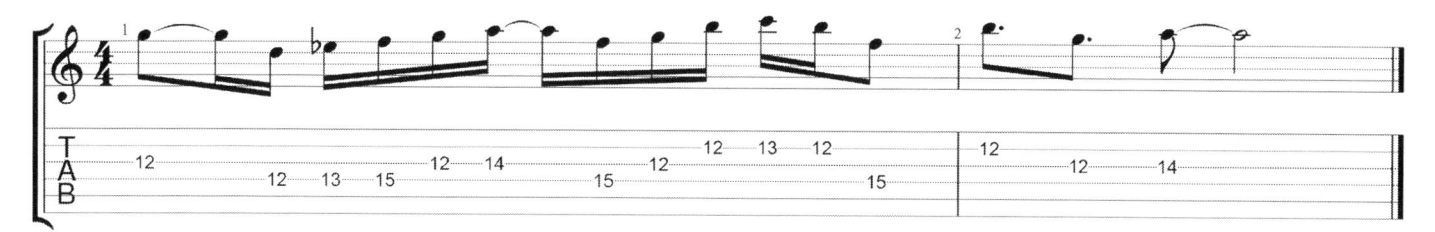

Example 5 | Track 41

Here we are resolving to the 3rd.

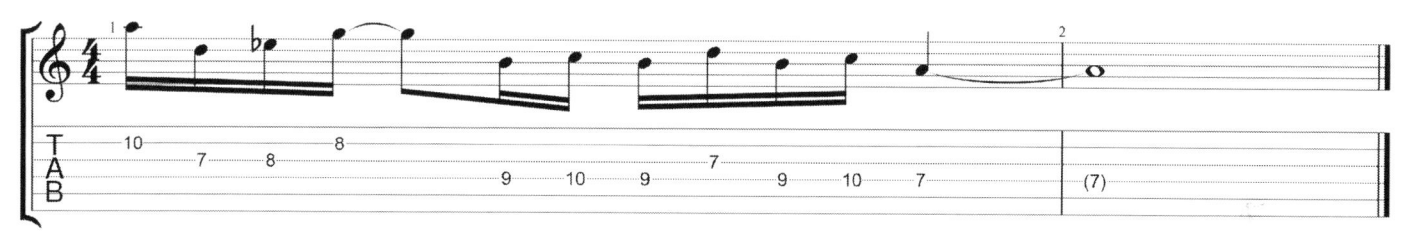

Example 6 | Track 42

This example is resolving to the 5th.

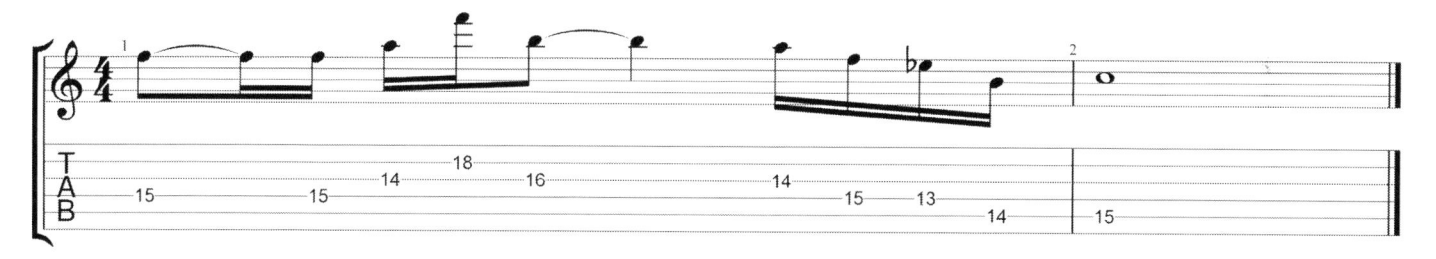

Next are some examples of the b7 'sweet note':

Example 7 | Track 43

This is resolving to the 5th.

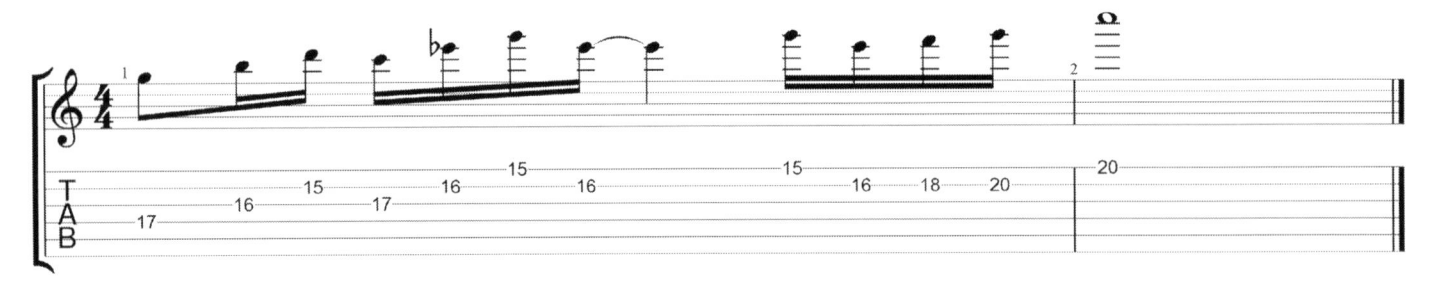

Example 8 | Track 44

Here we are resolving to the 5th.

Example 9 | Track 45

This is resolving to the 5th.

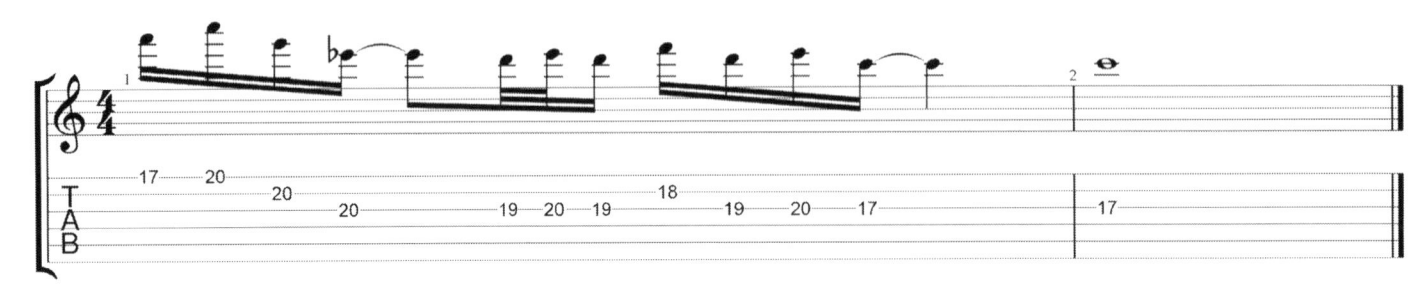

Apply It To Your Style

Now that you've been introduced to the Lydian Dominant mode, let's incorporate it into your playing. Remember that this mode can be used over V7 chords.

Beneath are some examples of F Lydian Dominant to be played over the standard rock backing track:

Example 10 | Track 46

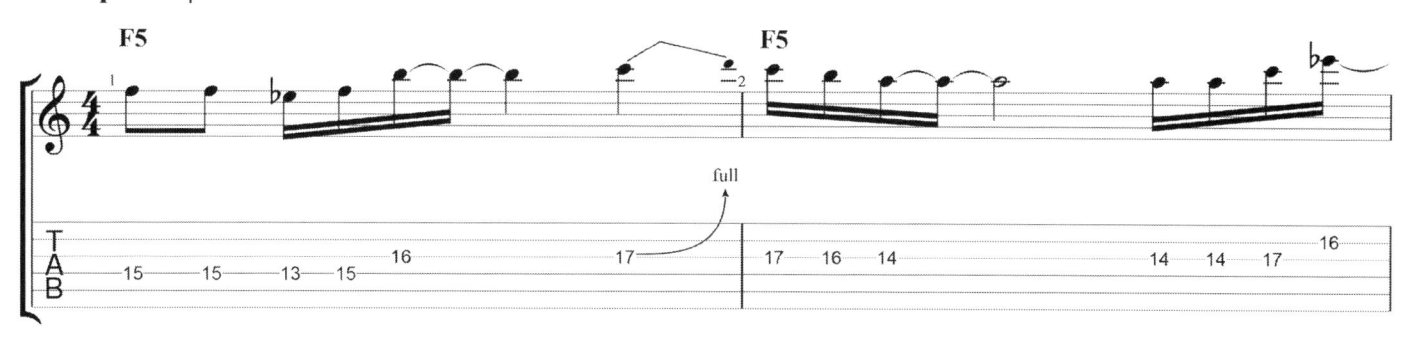

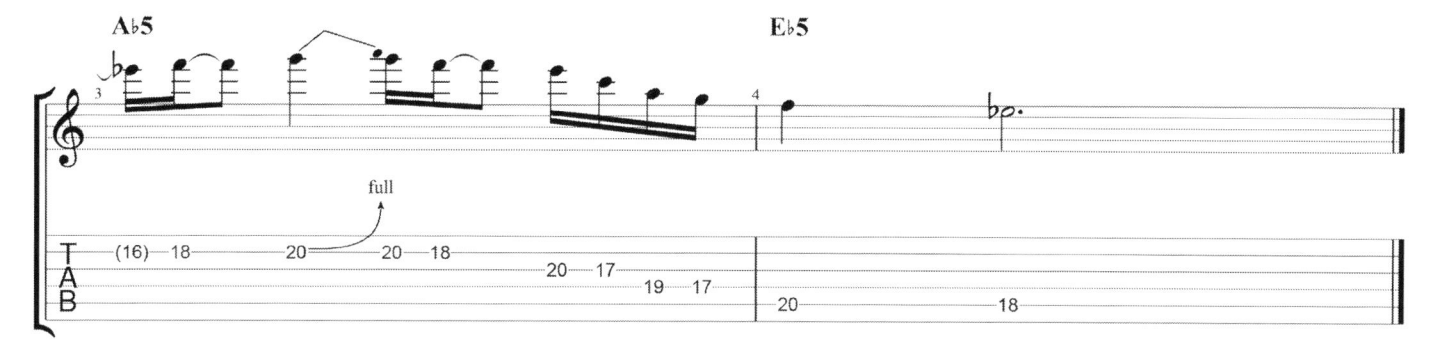

Example 11 | Track 47

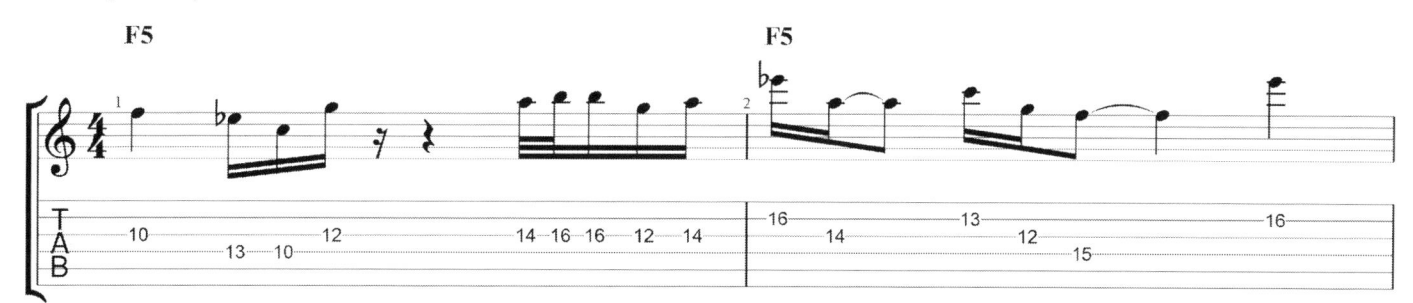

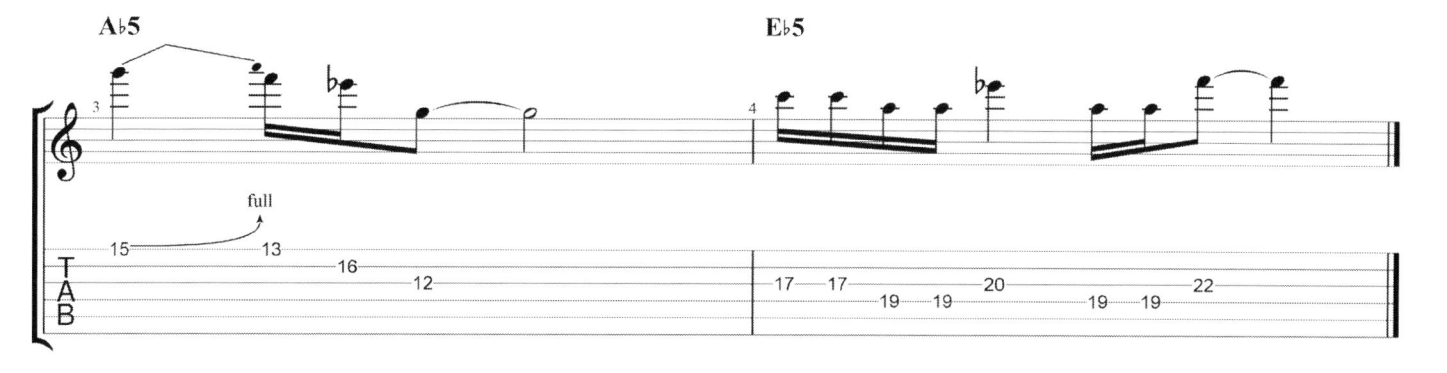

37

Example 12 | Track 48

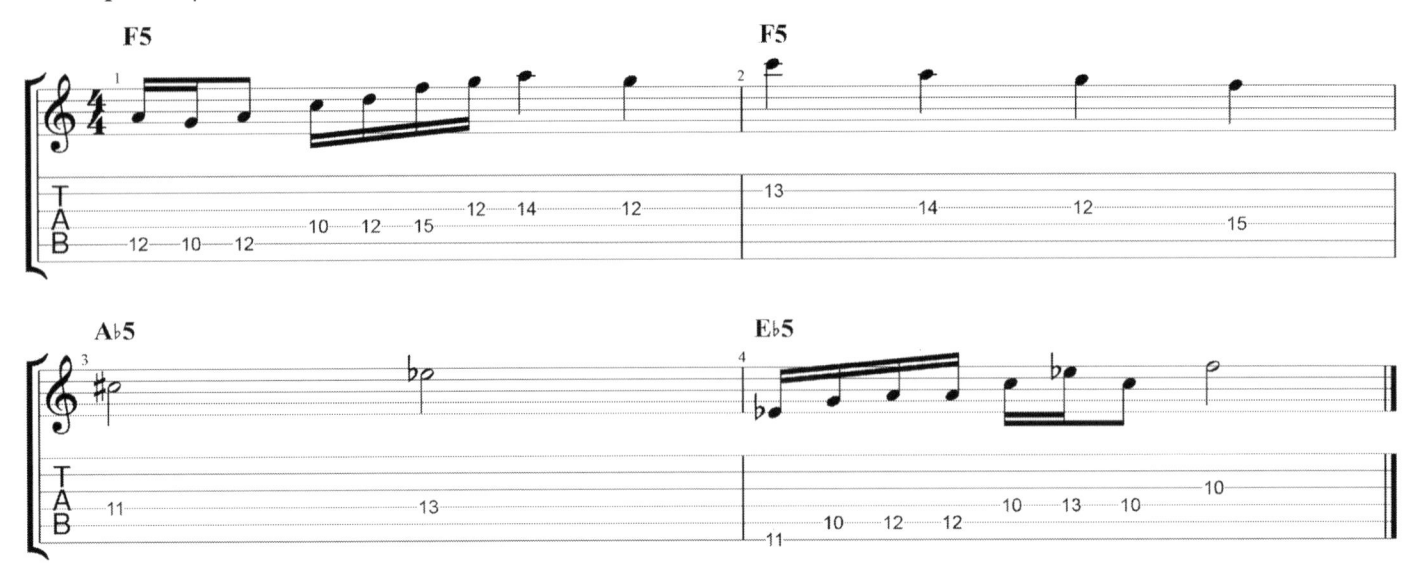

Example 13 | Track 49

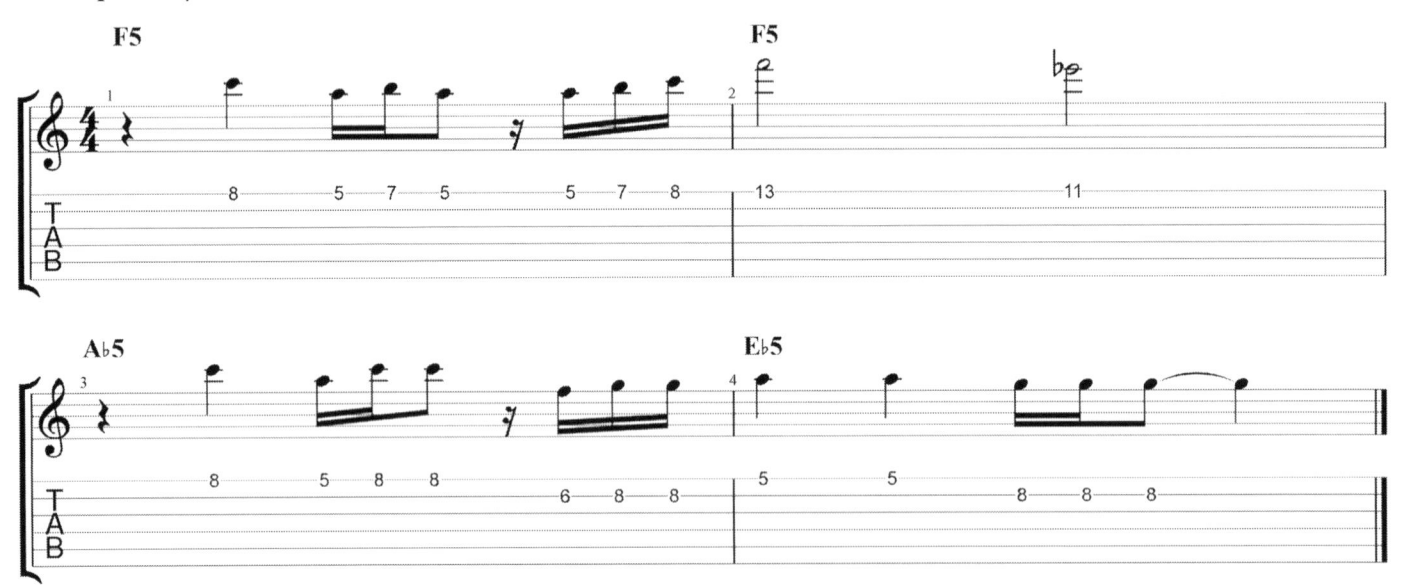

Food For Thought

A great way to help yourself to further understand the Melodic Minor Modes is to start linking the patterns you have learnt in previous chapters together. We suggest playing down C Melodic Minor, up D Dorian b2, down Eb Lydian #5, and then up F Lydian Dominant. With each new chapter, add that mode to this sequence.

If you are struggling with a mode in this book, make sure you revisit the arpeggio section of the chapter, as these are a good way of distinguishing the sound of this mode from the others. Take your time to practice your licks with a metronome as accuracy is always more important than speed. You can practice your licks over the backing tracks provided in the download.

G Mixolydian b6

5th Mode of C Melodic Minor

The Mixolydian b6 mode is, as the name suggests, a Mixolydian mode with a flattened 6th. It is another great mode to use over V7 chords. The key to successfully using this mode is getting a good balance between its major and minor elements, namely the major 3rd and b6th.

Mode Positions

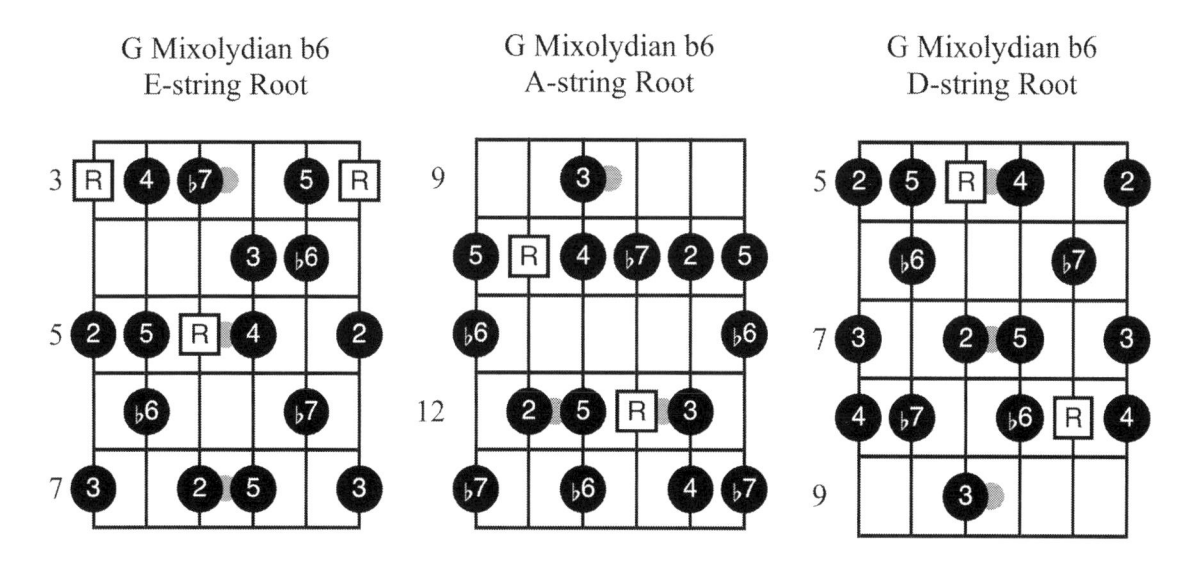

G Mixolydian b6
E-string Root

G Mixolydian b6
A-string Root

G Mixolydian b6
D-string Root

Practice these patterns to familiarise yourself with this mode. Play the mode over the V7b13 and V7 chords.

Chord Diagrams

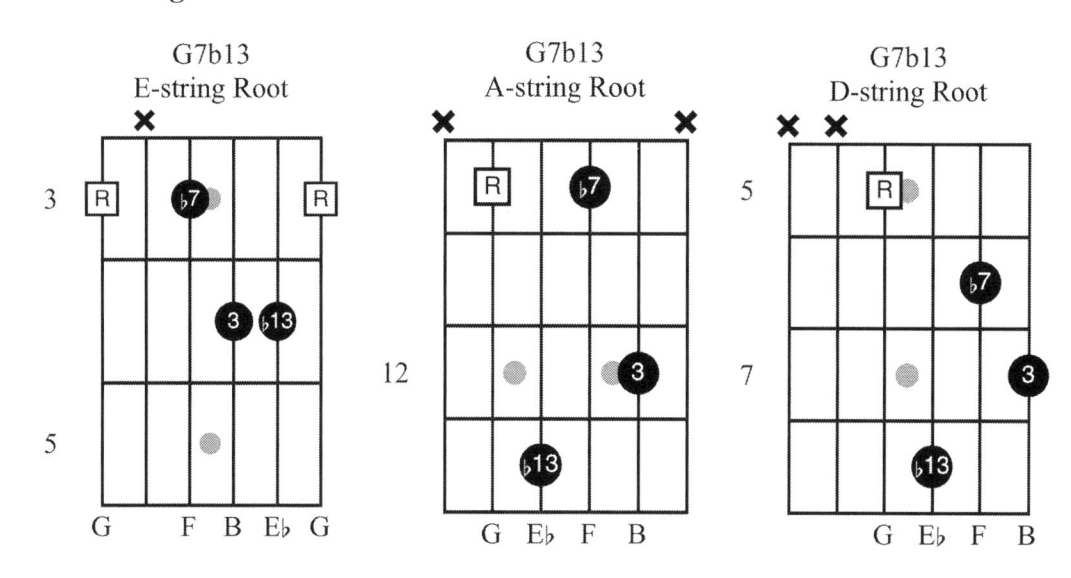

G7b13
E-string Root

G7b13
A-string Root

G7b13
D-string Root

The Mixolydian b6 mode can be used over V7b13 chords because they both contain b6th and b7th intervals.

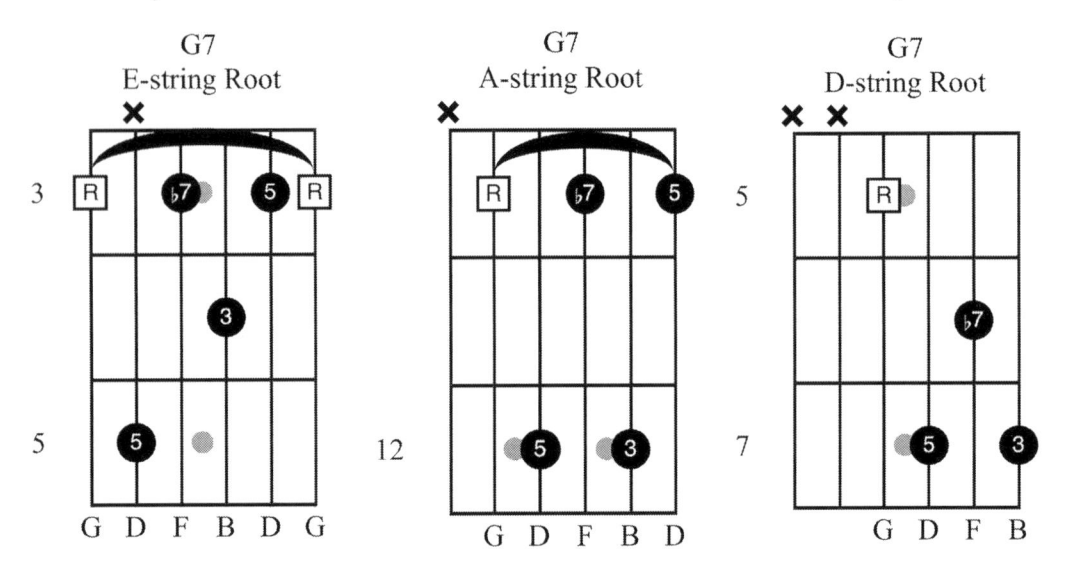

While the Mixolydian b6 mode sounds particularly good over V7b13 chords, it can also be used over standard V7 chords to add some tension.

Cooking With Arpeggios

The next thing to do in order to become familiar with the sound of the Mixolydian b6 mode is to play the arpeggio.

These are some G Mixolydian b6 arpeggios:

Example 1 | Track 50

G Mixolydian b6 arpeggio in root position. When moving between the major 3rd and b6th on the G and B strings, try not to get tripped up, it can be a difficult passage.

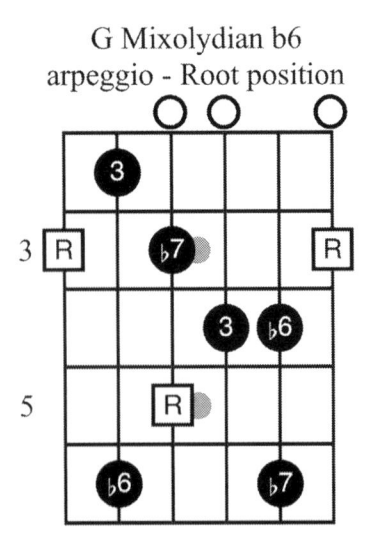

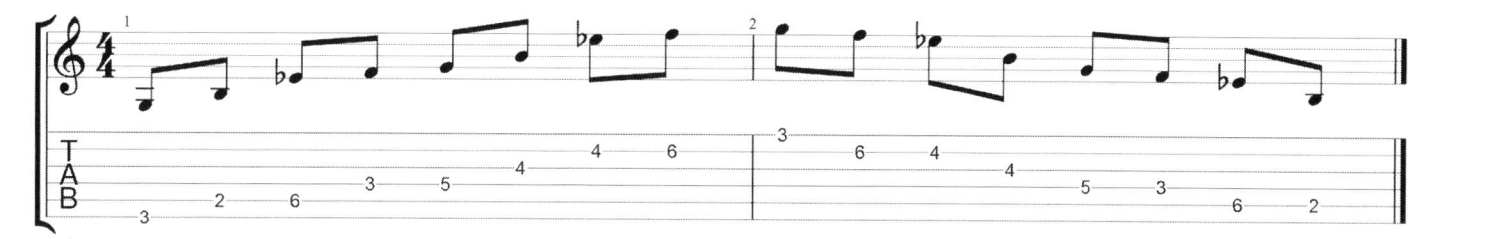

Example 2 | Track 51

G Mixolydian b6 arpeggio in 1st inversion. Be aware of the big stretch in this arpeggio.

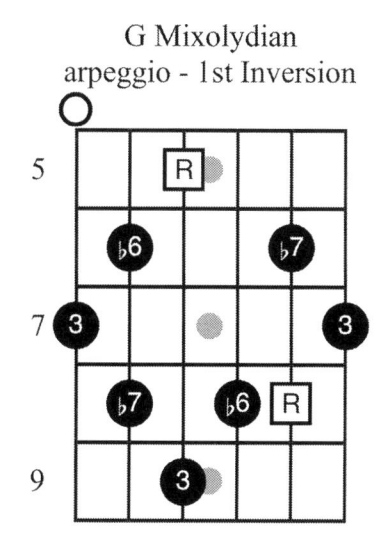

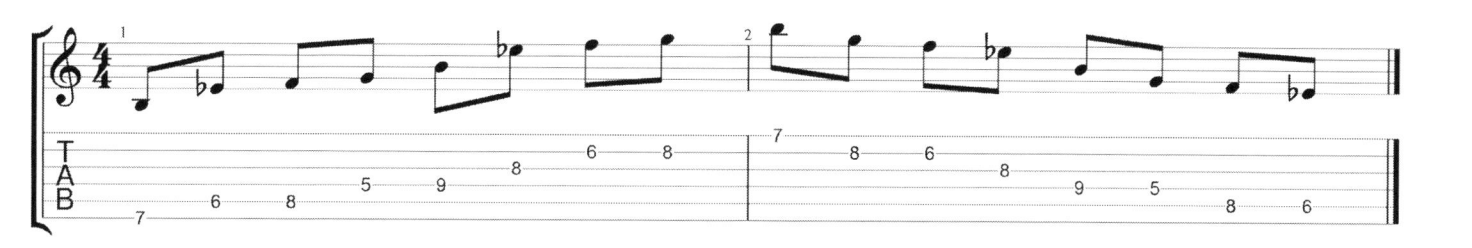

Example 3 | Track 52

G Mixolydian b6 arpeggio launched off the b6. This can be tricky as it is a combination of the stretch and the roll between the B and the G string.

G Mixolydian b6
arpeggio - Launching
from b6

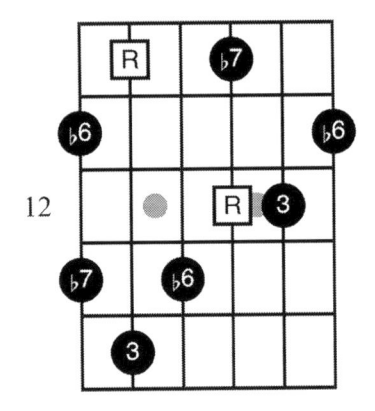

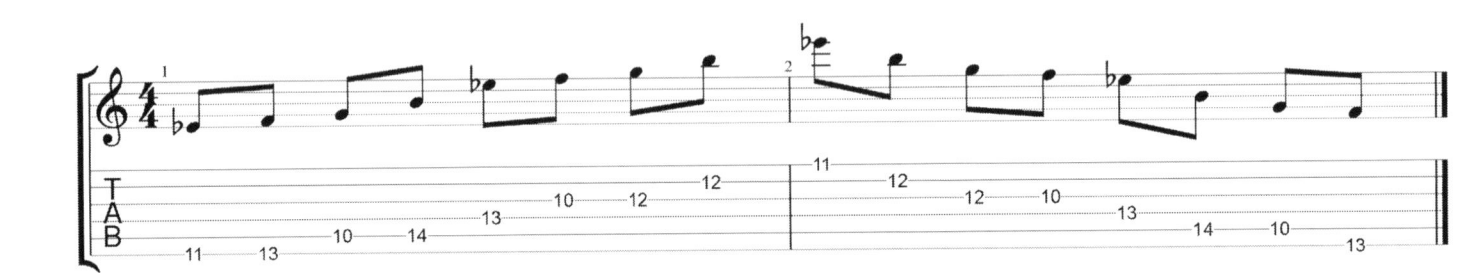

Practice these patterns over the backing track provided at the end of each example on the free audio download. Use these arpeggios as starting points for writing your own solos.

Targeting The Sweet Notes

The 'sweet notes' of the Mixolydian b6 mode are the major 3rd and b6th; in this case they will be B and Eb. To bring out the flavour of the Mixolydian b6 mode we need to have a balance between these 'sweet notes'. Try not to favour one 'sweet note' over the other as you can risk sounding one-dimensional.

Below are some examples of the major 3rd 'sweet note':

Example 4 | Track 53

In this example we are targeting the major 3rd 'sweet note'. One effective way of getting to the B is by utilising the C.

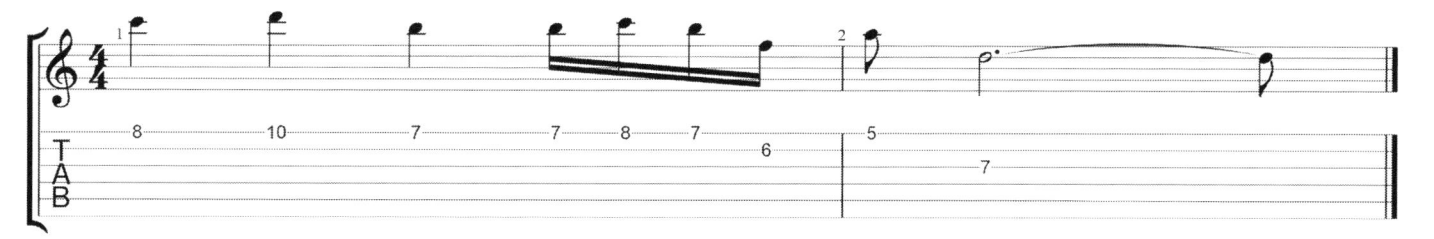

Example 5 | Track 54

Here we are resolving to the 2nd.

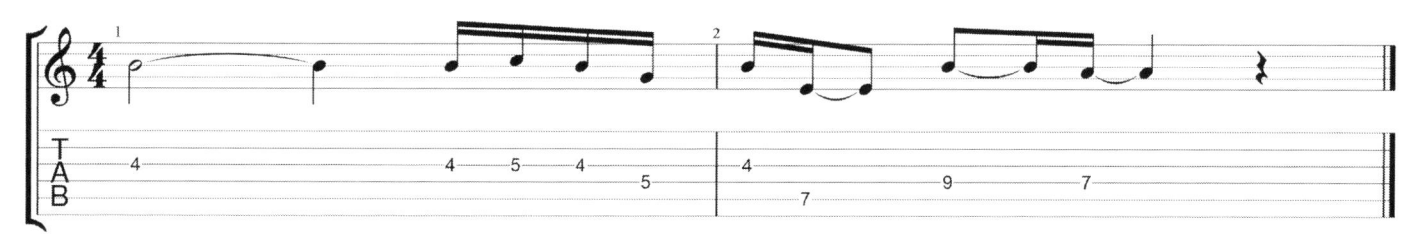

Example 6 | Track 55

This example is resolving to the 3rd.

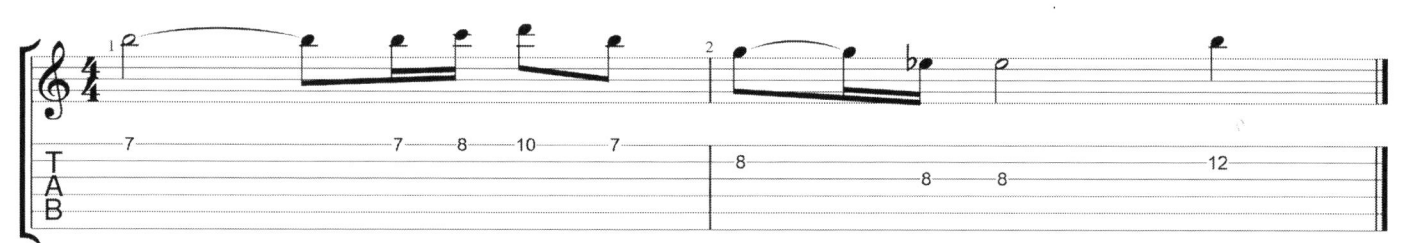

Next are some examples of the b6 'sweet note':

Example 7 | Track 56

Here we are resolving to the 3rd.

Example 8 | Track 57

This is resolving to the 5th.

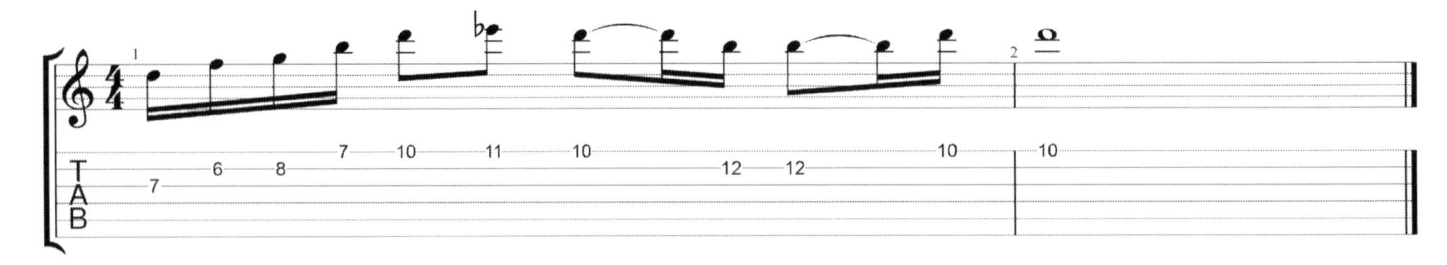

Example 9 | Track 58

Here we are resolving to the 5th.

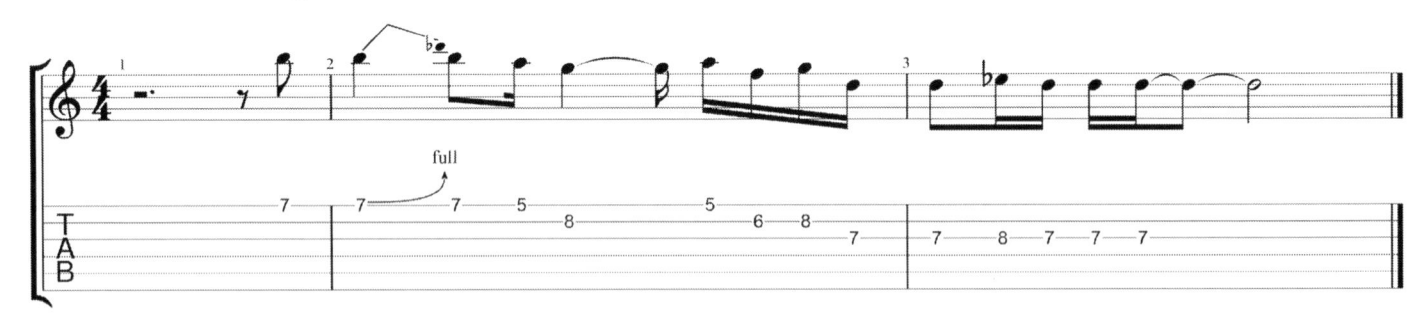

Apply It To Your Style

Now that you're becoming familiar with the Mixolydian b6 mode, it's time to integrate it into your playing.

Remember not to favour one 'sweet note' over the other.

Beneath are some examples of G Mixolydian b6 to be played over the standard rock backing track:

Example 10 | Track 59

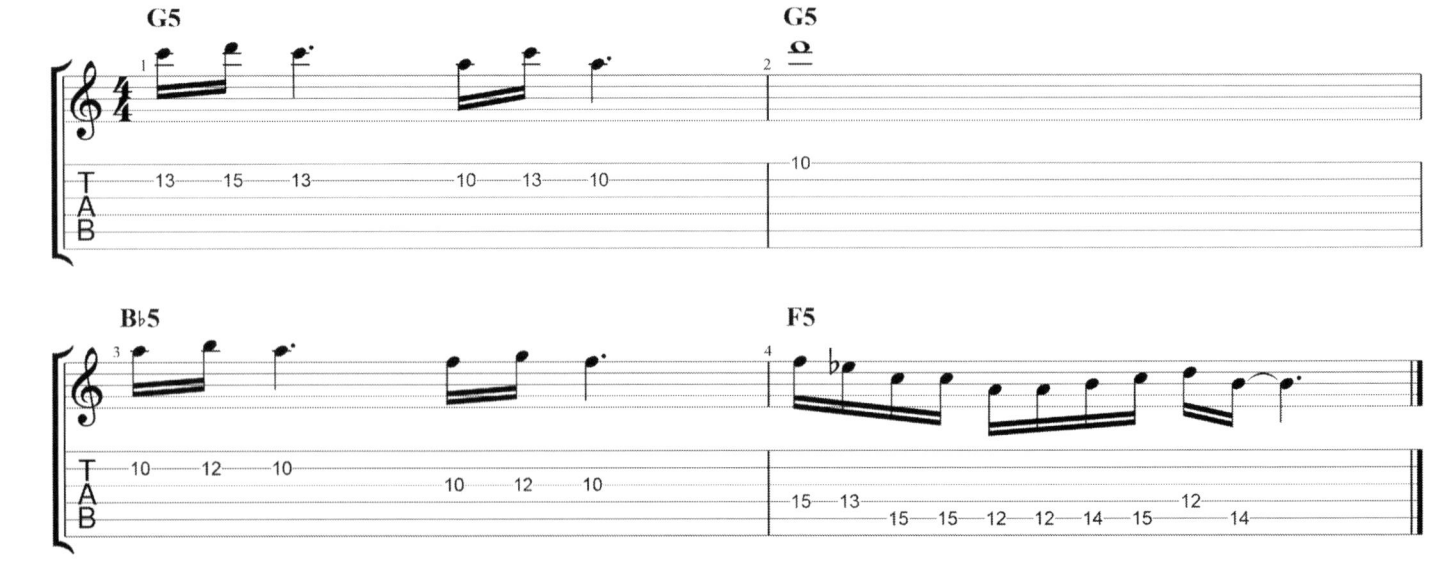

Example 11 | Track 60

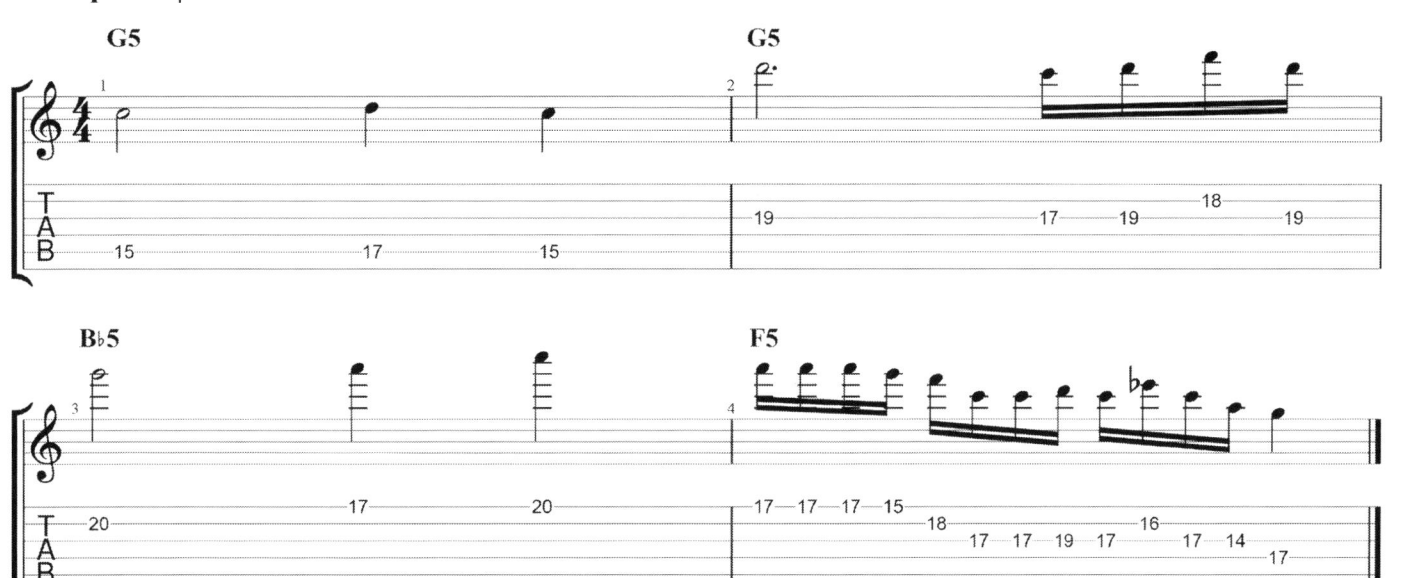

Example 12 | Track 61

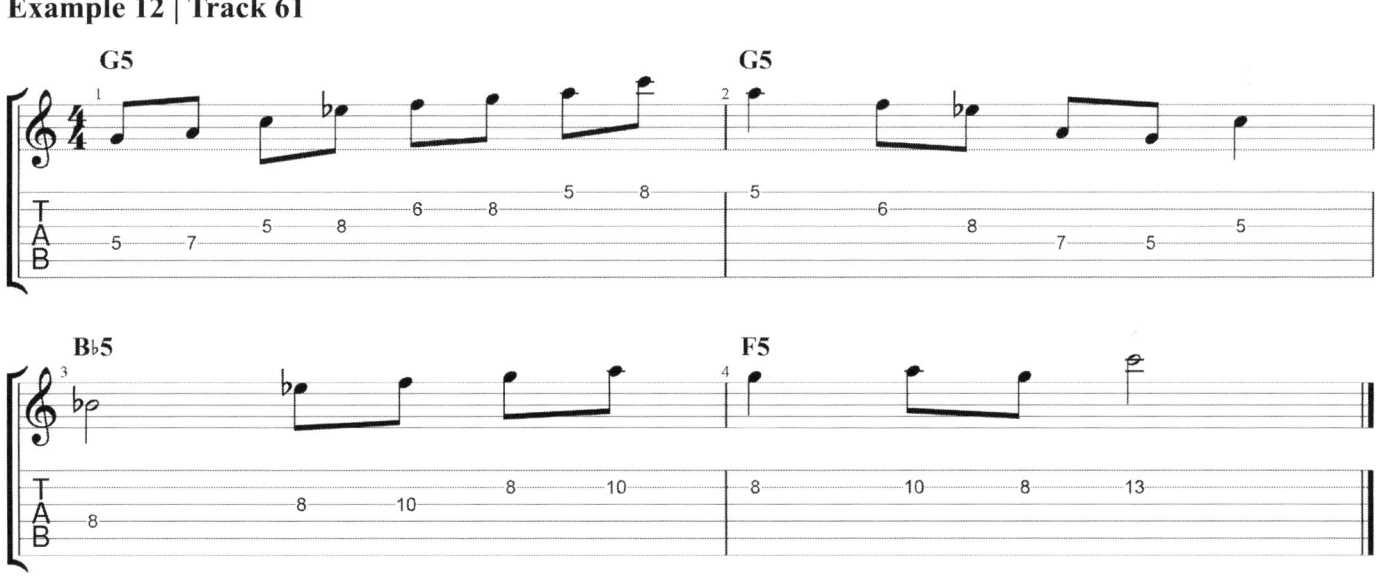

Example 13 | Track 62

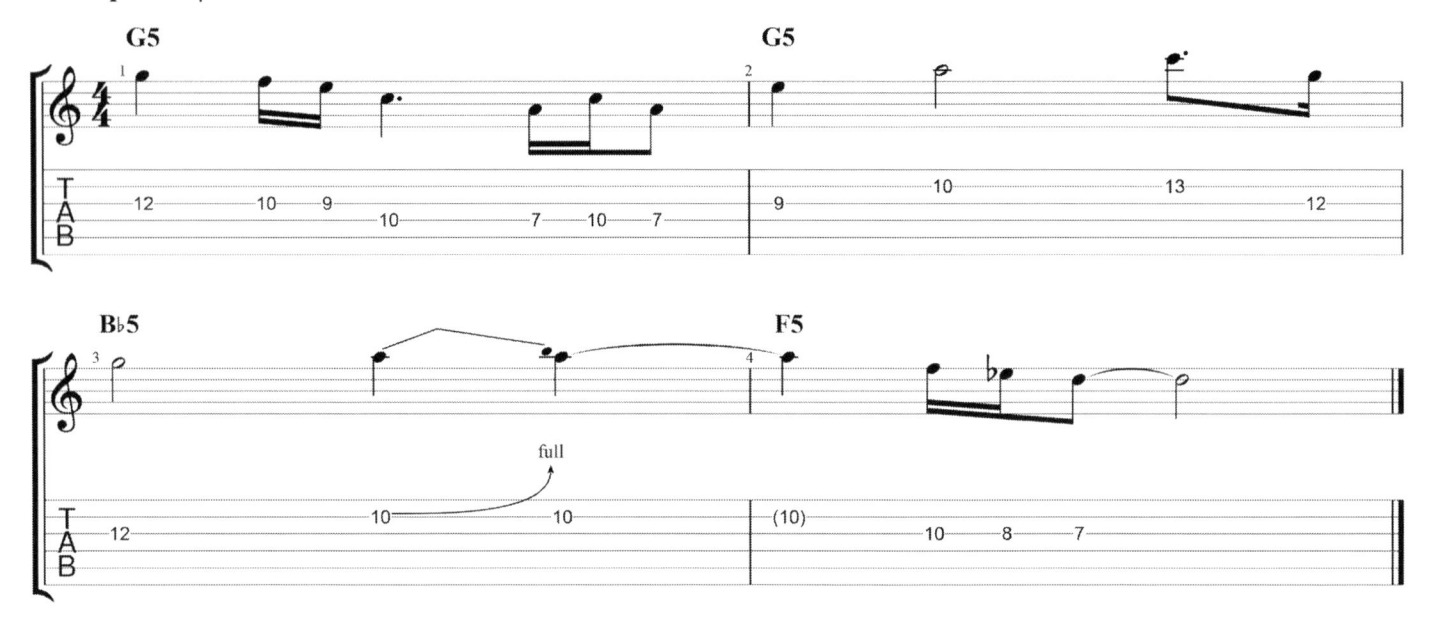

Now that you have another mode under your belt, add it to the sequence of modes to practice.

Continue to practice your musical ideas over the backing tracks provided. Try to see if you can use other modes from previous chapters alongside each other. Figure out which modes you think work well together and which ones don't. Try taking some of the concepts learnt in this chapter and play them over your favourite songs.

A Aeolian b5

6th Mode of C Melodic Minor

The Aeolian b5 mode is as the name suggests, an Aeolian mode with a flattened 5th. It is also referred to as the Locrian Natural 2 mode. You may find the sound of the Aeolian b5 mode familiar, as it partially resembles the blues scale. They are both minor scales that contain a b5 which add a sense of chromaticism to the mode.

Mode Positions

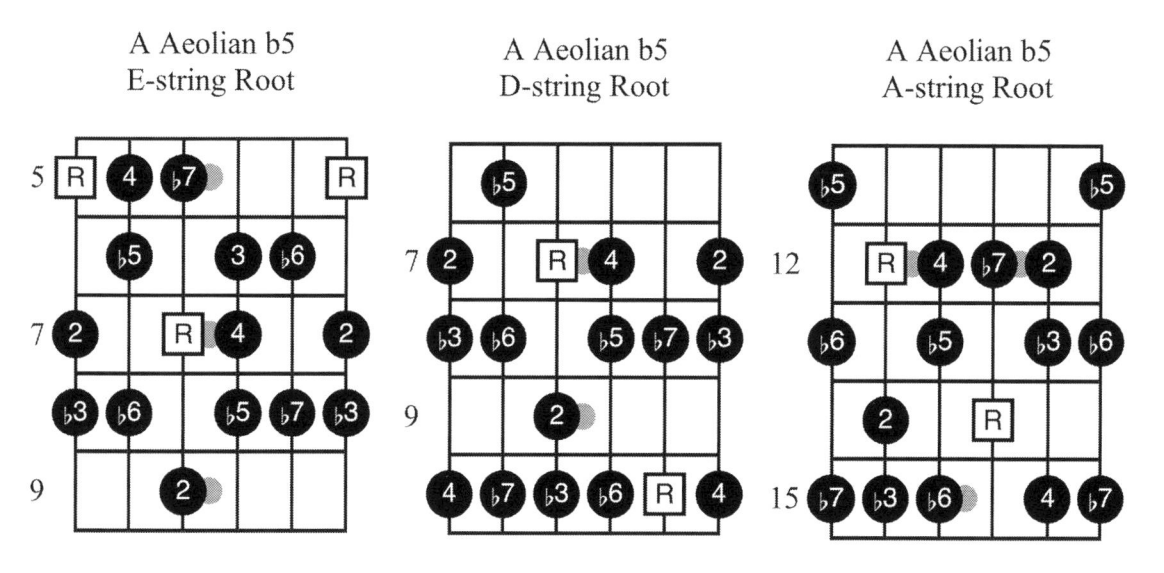

Practice these patterns to familiarise yourself with this mode. Play the mode over the minor7b5 and minor7 chords.

Chord Diagrams

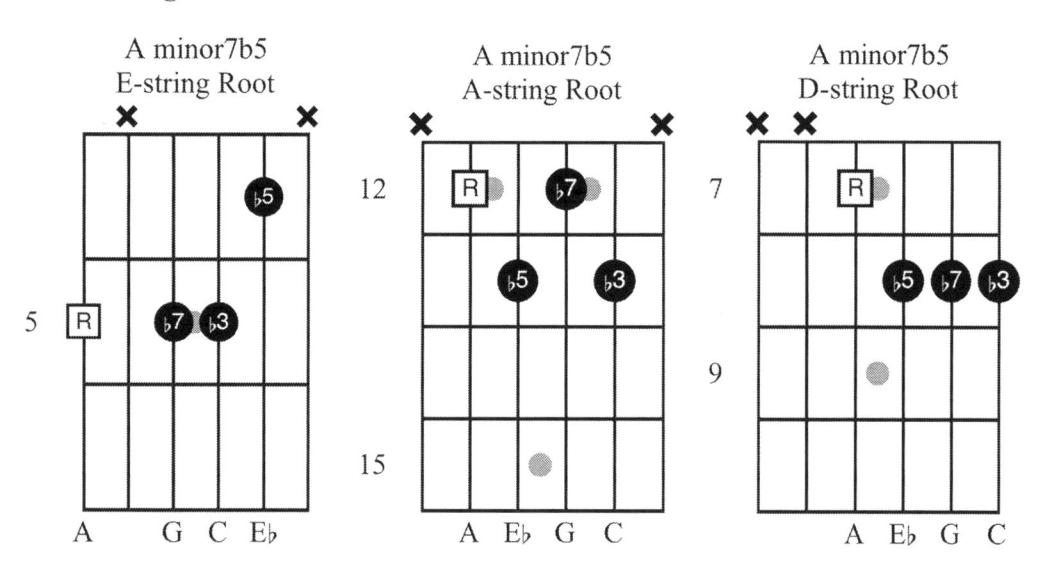

The Aeolian b5 mode is commonly used over m7b5 chords, which are often found as the ii chord in minor ii, v, i progressions. These chords are found more often in jazz music than in rock or pop.

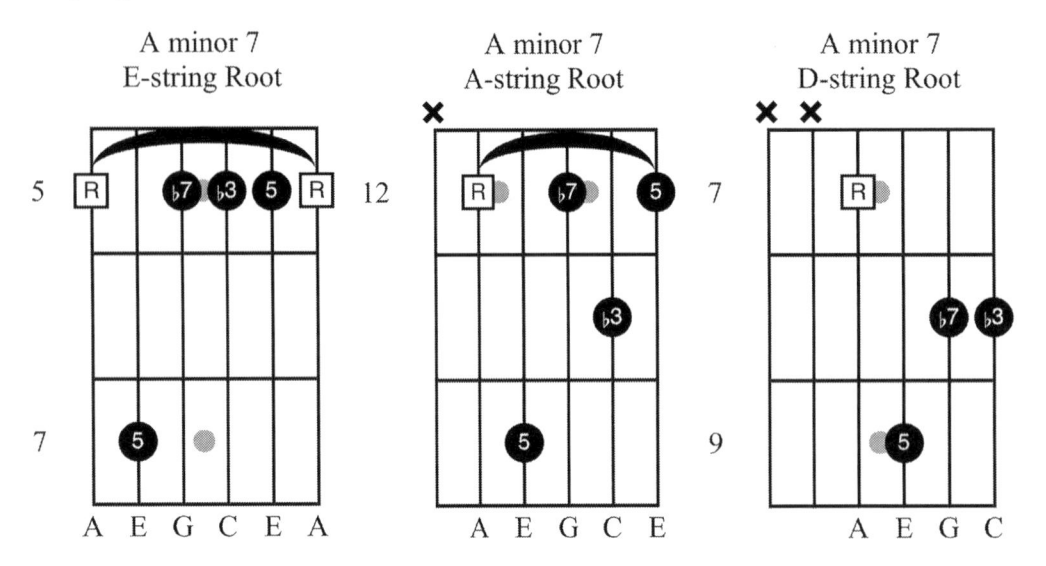

The Aeolian b5 mode will still work over minor7 chords, as they have minor 3rd and b7th scale degrees in common.

Cooking With Arpeggios

The next step to take in order to become familiar with the sound of the Aeolian b5 mode is to play the arpeggio.

These are some A Aeolian b5 arpeggios:

Example 1 | Track 63

A Aeolian b5 arpeggio in root position. Try not to get tripped up on the G and B strings as it can be a difficult passage.

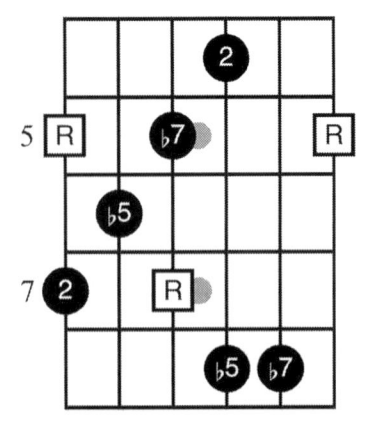

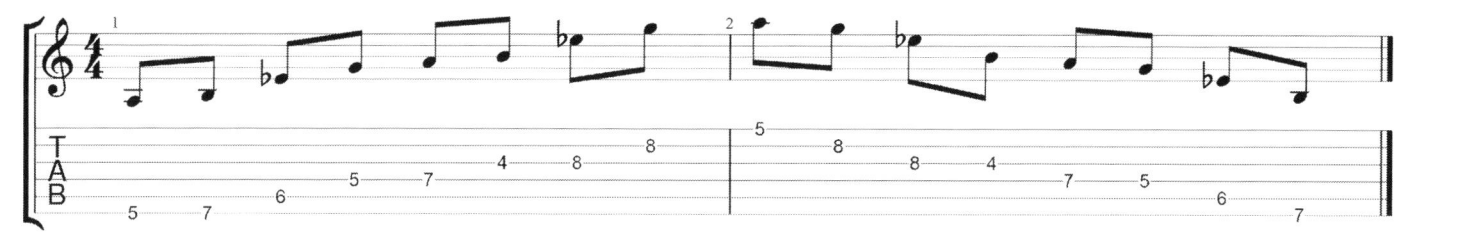

Example 2 | Track 64

A Aeolian b5 arpeggio launched off the 2nd. Be aware of the big stretch in this arpeggio. Start slow and work your way up to speed.

49

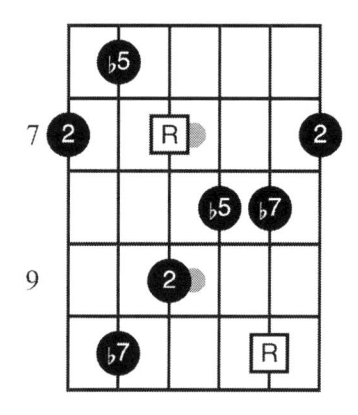

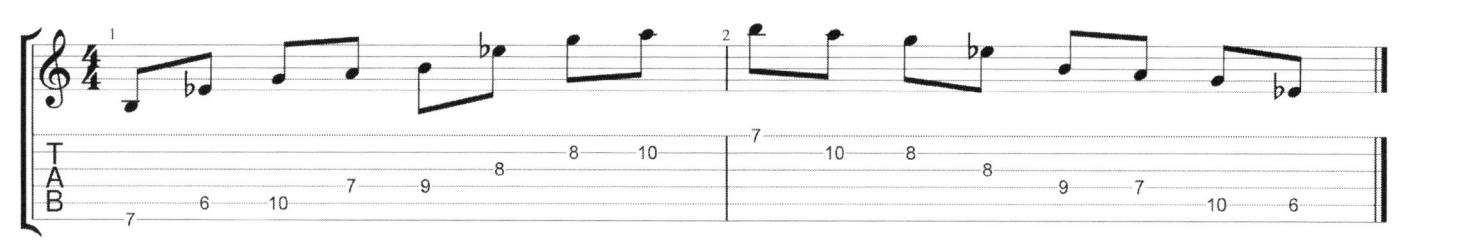

Example 3 | Track 65

A Aeolian b5 arpeggio in 2nd inversion. You may have noticed this is the same shape as the Mixolydian b6 arpeggio in 1st inversion.

A Aeolian b5
arpeggio - 2nd Inversion

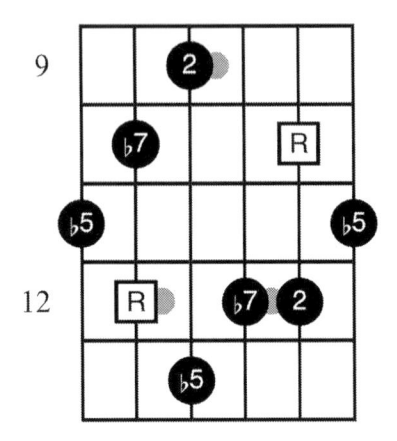

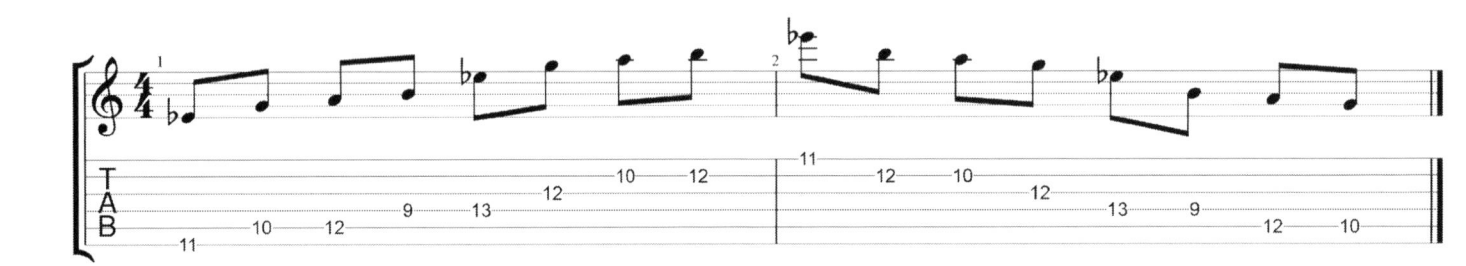

Practice these patterns over the backing track provided at the end of each example on the free audio download. Use these arpeggios as starting points for writing your own solos.

Targeting The Sweet Notes

The 'sweet note' in the A Aeolian b5 mode is the b5

The trick for dealing with the b5 is in the resolution of the note. One way we found very effective was to resolve the b5 down to the minor 3rd. In this case it would be resolving the Eb down to a C. You don't want to be caught sitting on the b5 for too long because unresolved dissonance can become directionless.

Below are some examples of the b5 'sweet note':

Example 4 | Track 66

Here we are resolving to the 7th.

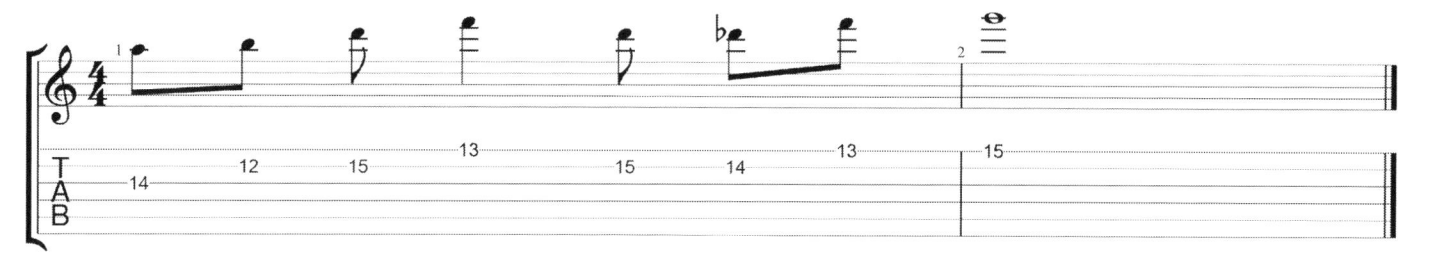

Example 5 | Track 67

This example is resolving to the 2nd.

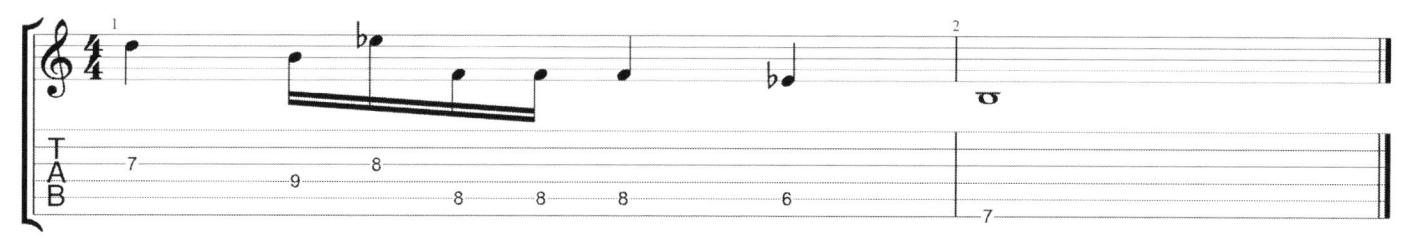

Example 6 | Track 68

This is resolving to the 3rd.

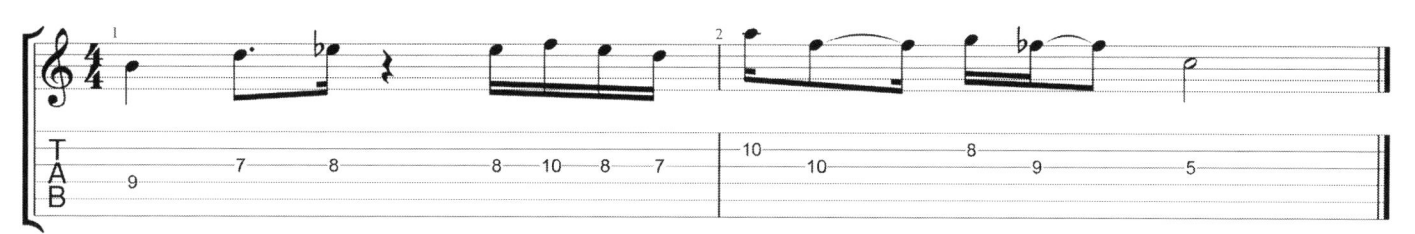

Apply It To Your Style

Now that you're beginning to the grasp the Aeolian b5 mode, it's time to integrate it into your playing. Remember that this mode can be used over standard minor7 chords as well as minor7b5 chords.

Next are some examples of the A Aeolian b5 mode to be played over the standard rock backing track:

Example 7 | Track 69

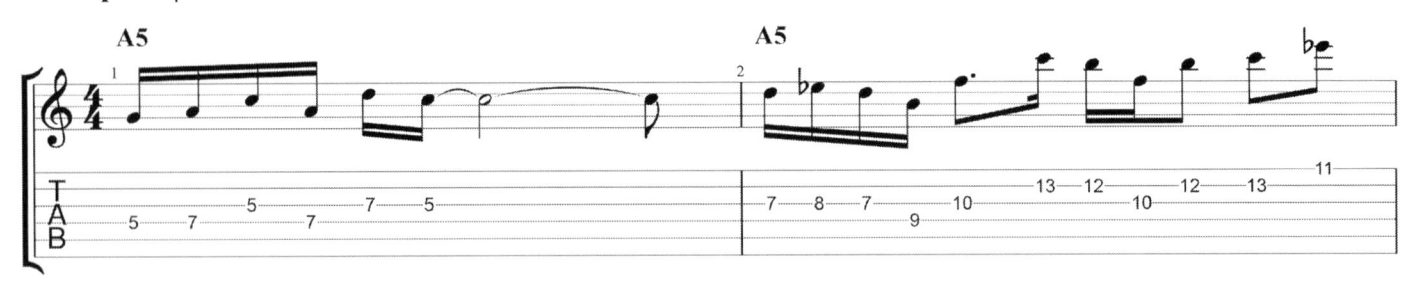

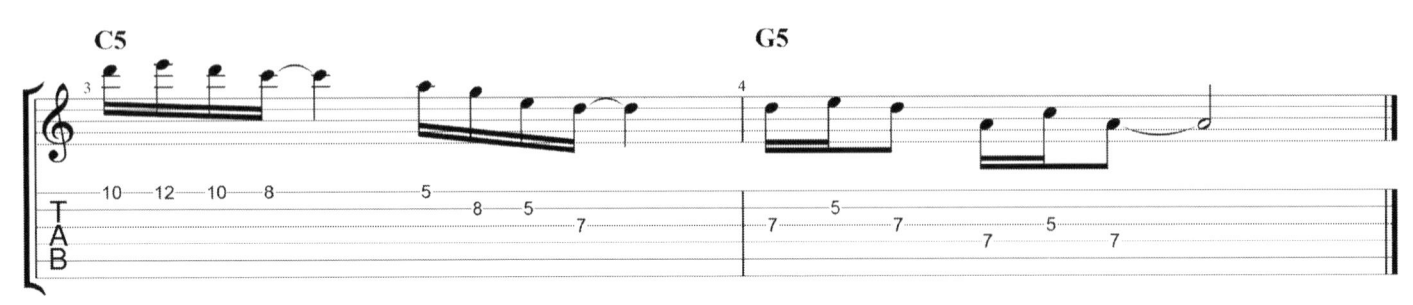

Example 8 | Track 70

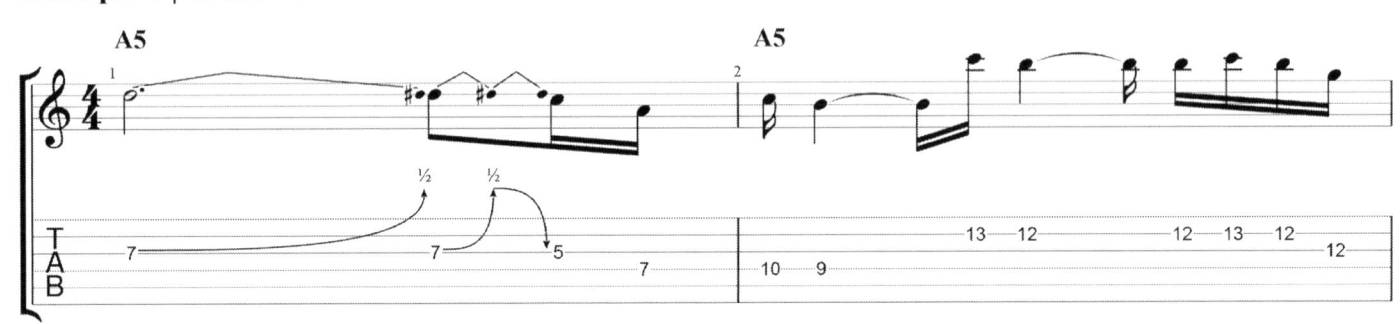

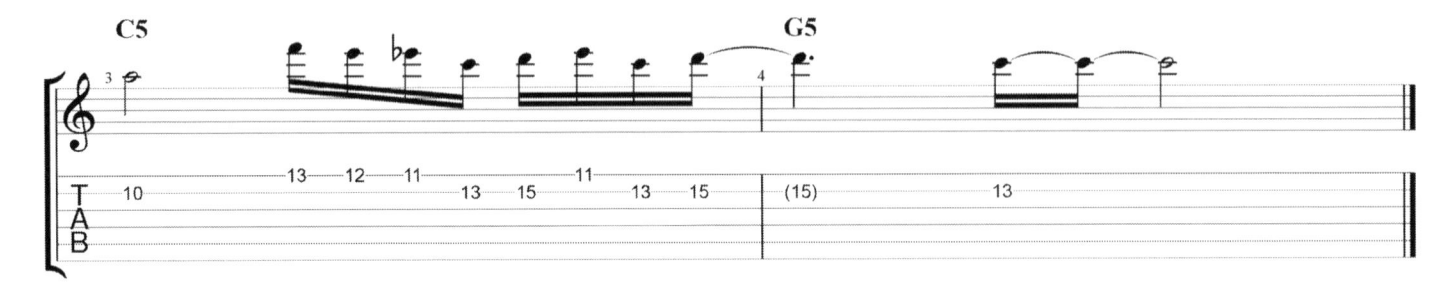

Example 9 | Track 71

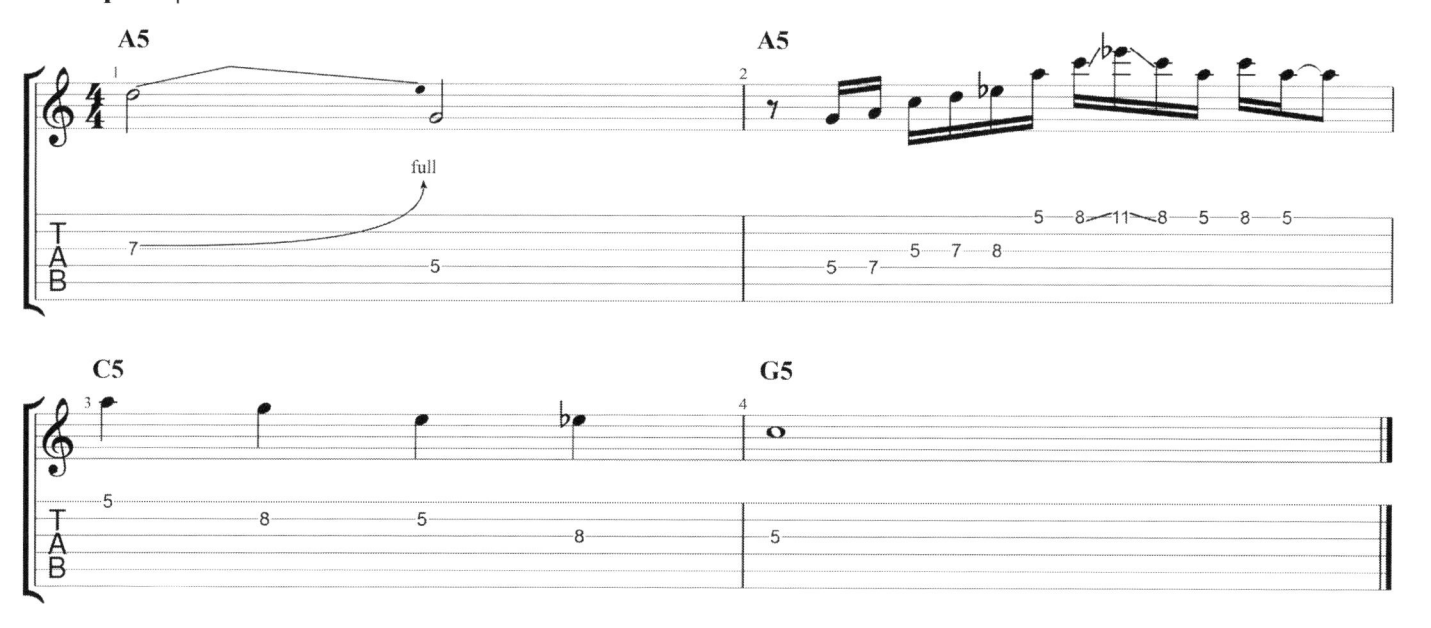

Now that you have another mode under your belt, add it to the sequence of modes to practice.

We've now covered a lot of content. The best way to deal with the amount of information is to choose a few of your favourite ideas and incorporate them into your practice. Practice working these ideas up over the backing tracks provided at the end of each audio download. Over time they will become a natural part of your playing.

B Super Locrian

7th Mode of C Melodic Minor

The Super Locrian mode is a very useful tool for adding tensions to V7 chords. It is also known as the Altered scale because of the altered notes it contains; b2, b3, b4, b5, b6, and b7.

Mode Positions

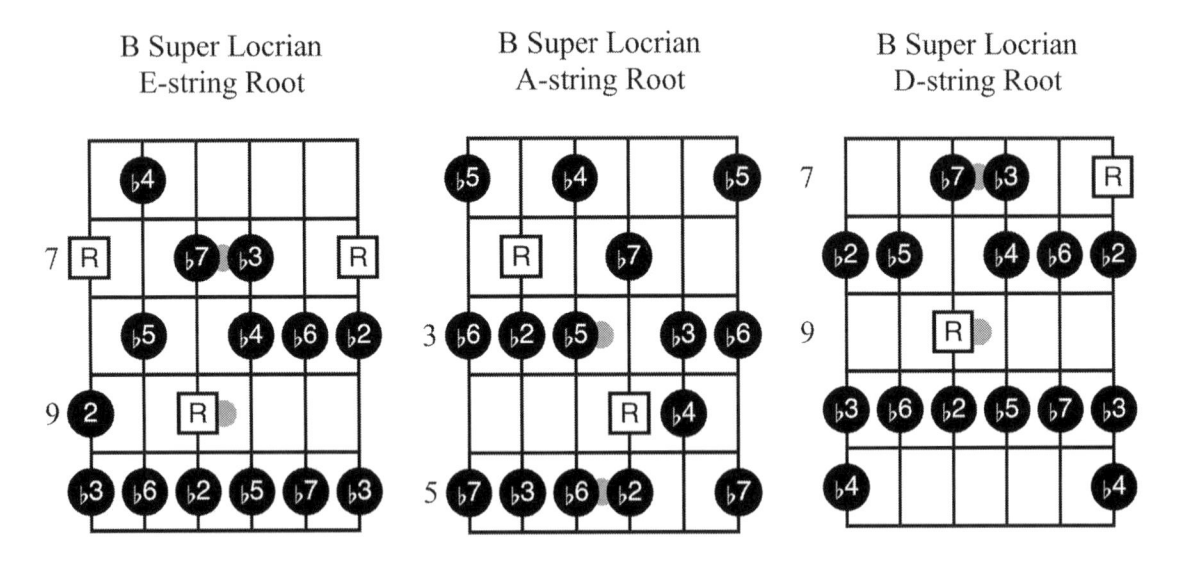

B Super Locrian E-string Root

B Super Locrian A-string Root

B Super Locrian D-string Root

Chord Diagrams

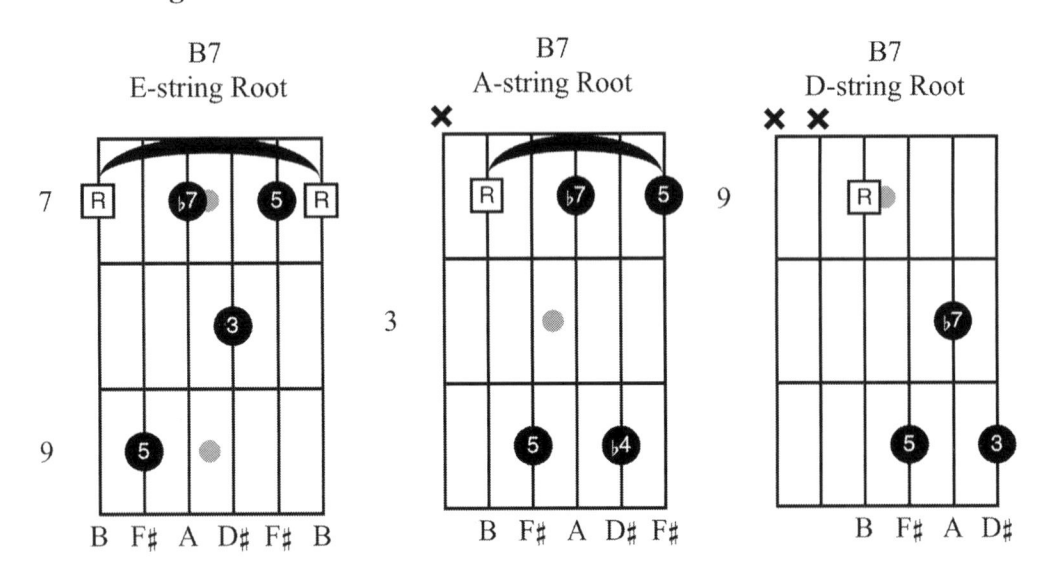

B7 E-string Root
B F# A D# F# B

B7 A-string Root
B F# A D# F#

B7 D-string Root
B F# A D#

54

B7b9
E-string Root

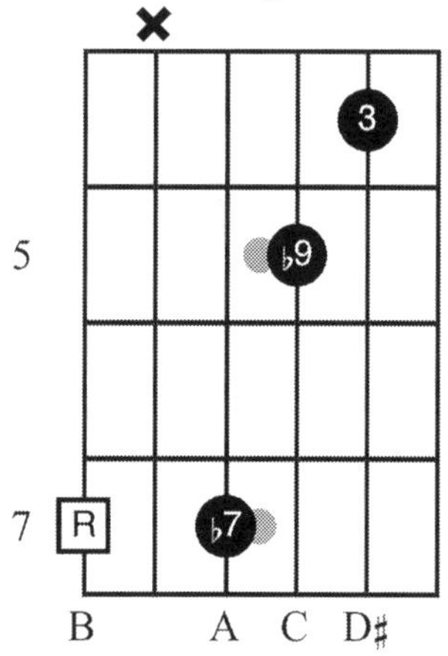

B7b9
A-string Root

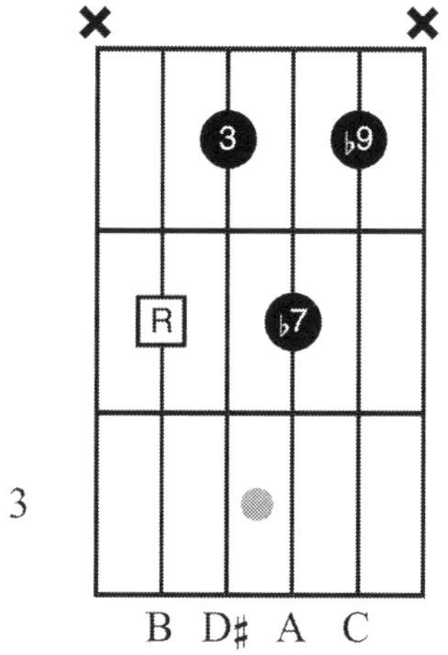

B7b9
D-string Root

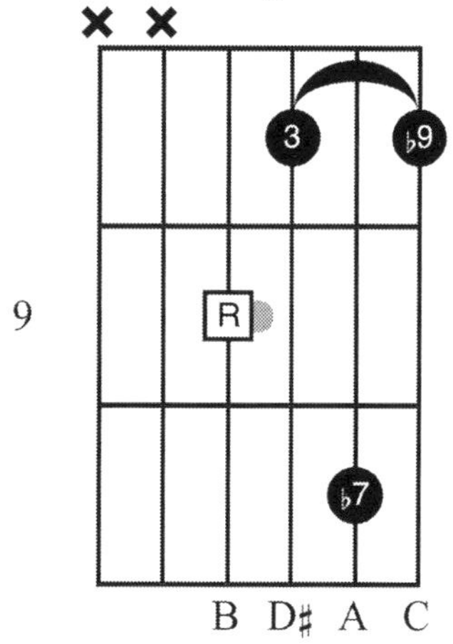

B7#9
E-string Root

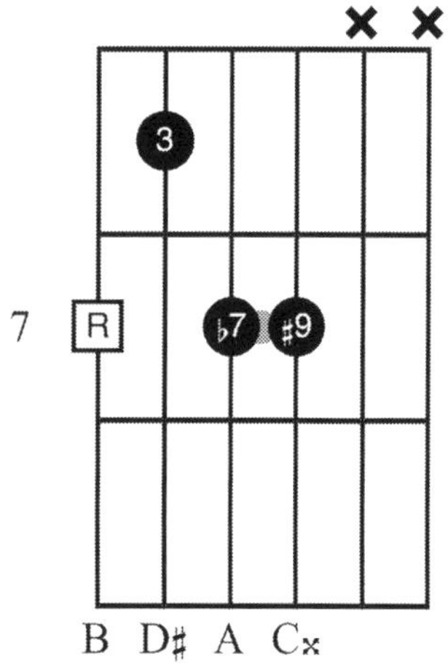

B7#9
A-string Root

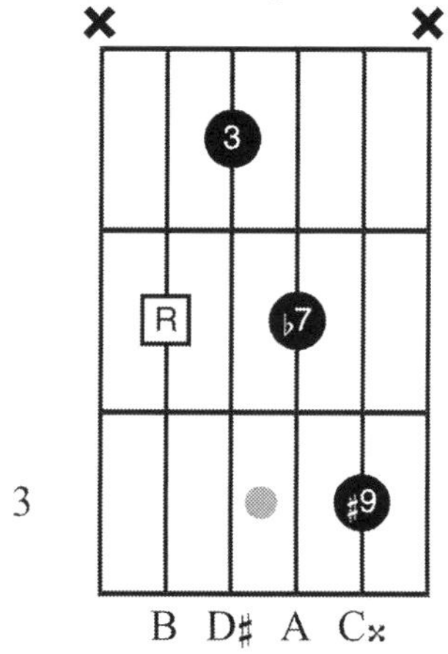

B7#9
D-string Root

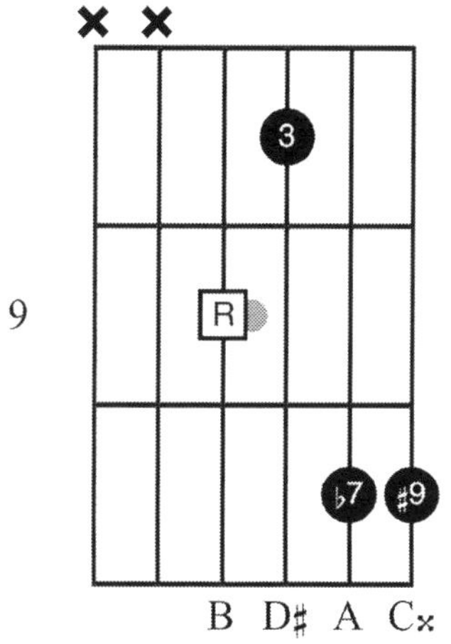

B7b5
E-string Root

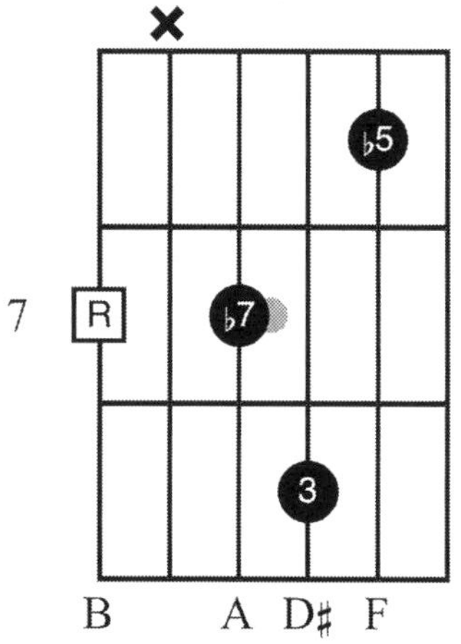

B7b5
A-string Root

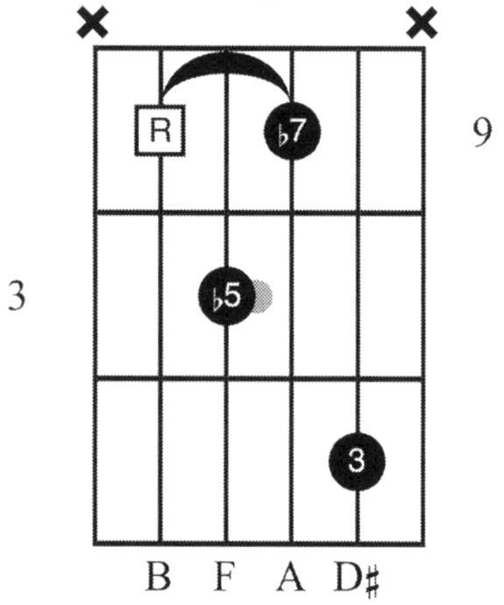

B7b5
D-string Root

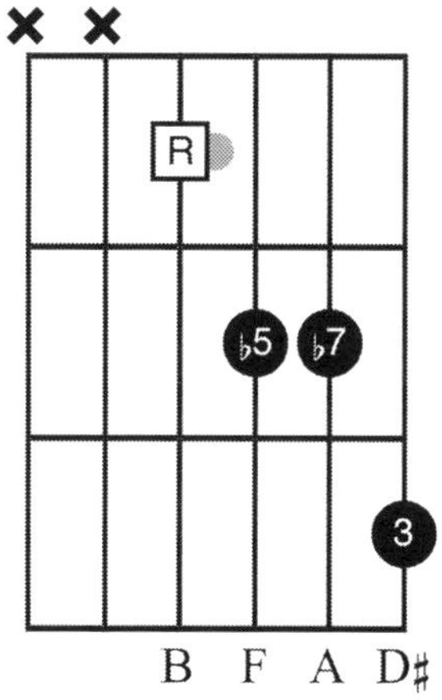

```
        B7#5                    B7#5                    B7#5
     E-string Root           A-string Root           D-string Root
```

[Chord diagrams for B7#5 in three positions]

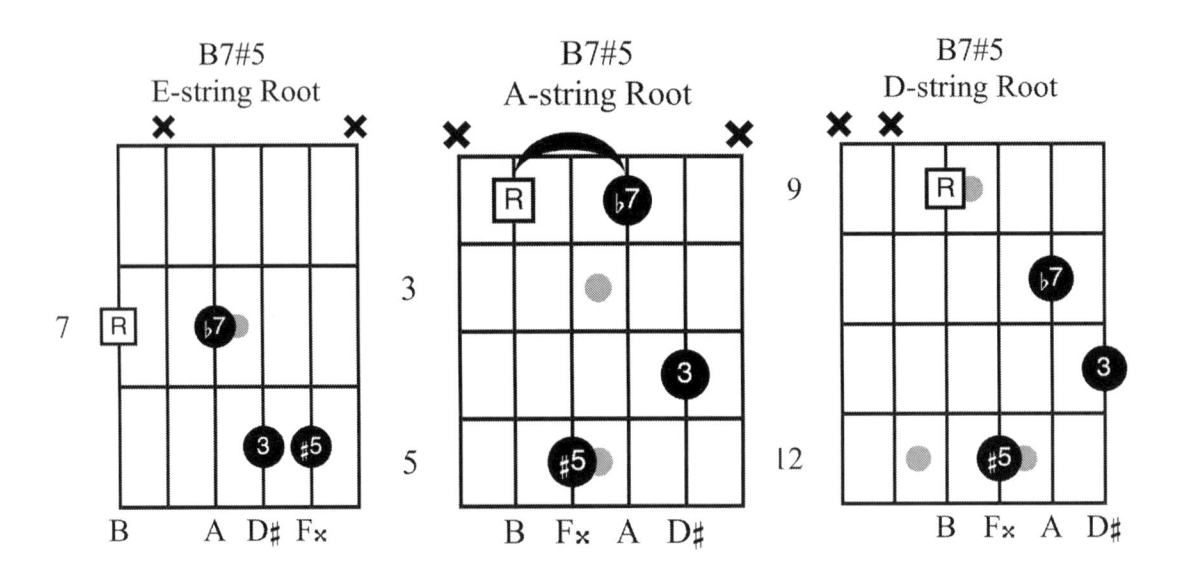

While in the world of jazz it is very common for the Super Locrian mode to be used over altered 7 chords, it also works equally well over unaltered 7 chords. This is because the altered notes in the mode add altered tensions to the V7 chords. These tensions are outlined clearly in the arpeggios.

Cooking With Arpeggios

The next thing to do in order to become familiar with the sound of the Super Locrian mode is to play the arpeggio.

Here are some B Super Locrian arpeggios:

Example 1 | Track 72

B Super Locrian arpeggio in root position. You will have to adjust your hand postition to be able to play this. We suggest sliding from the b7 to the root on the D string.

B Super Locrian
arpeggio - Root position

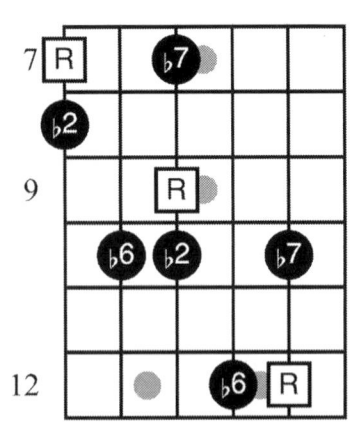

[Scale diagram]

56

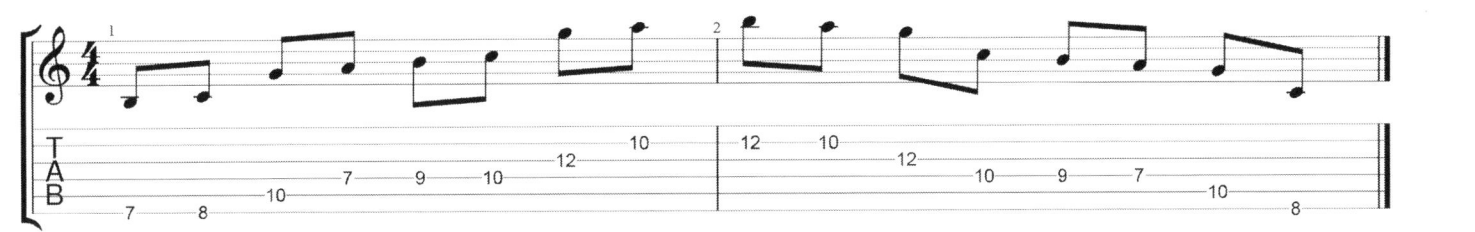

Example 2 | Track 73

B Super Locrian arpeggio launched off the b2nd. This has the same position shift as the previous example. Again, a slide will make this easier.

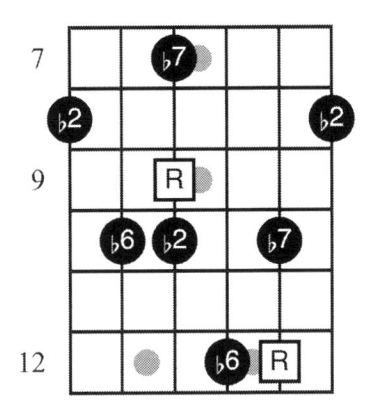

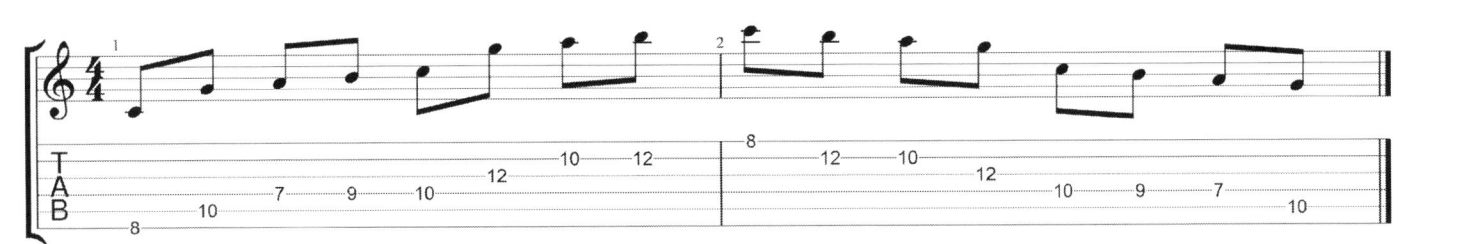

Example 3 | Track 74

B Super Locrian arpeggio launched off the b6th This arpeggio is difficult because there are a lot of one note per string passages. Pay attention to your pick direction.

B Super Locrian arpeggio - Launching from b6

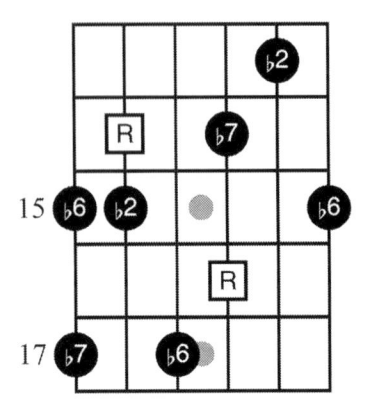

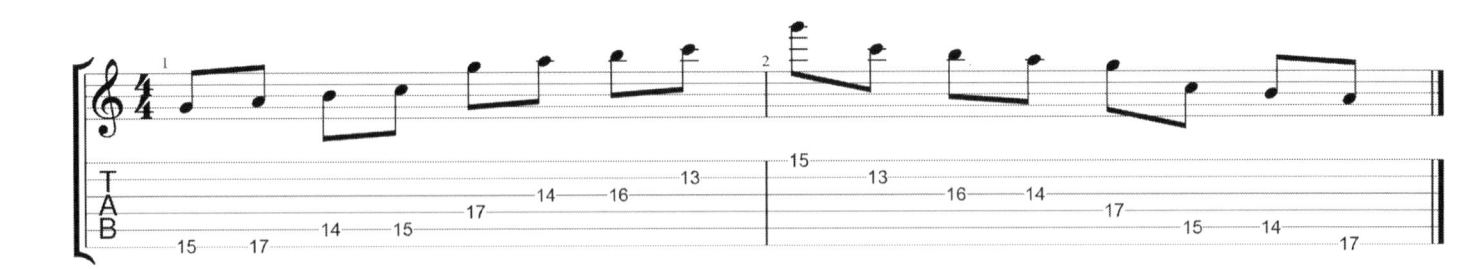

When playing these arpeggios, pay attention to how the altered tensions sound against the chord.

Practice these patterns over the backing track provided at the end of each example on the free audio download. Use these arpeggios as starting points for writing your own solos.

Targeting The Sweet Notes

The 'sweet notes' in the Super Locrian mode are the b9, #9, #11, and b13. The reason why we didn't include any other 'sweet notes' is because they are already present or at least implied in V7 chords. We treat these 'sweet notes' differently to others we have seen in previous chapters, because each Super Locrian 'sweet note' will add a different altered tension to V7 chords. It's best to focus on one 'sweet note' at a time, and develop that particular sound into our lines.

These are some examples of the b9 'sweet note':

Example 4 | Track 75

Here we are resolving to the b7th

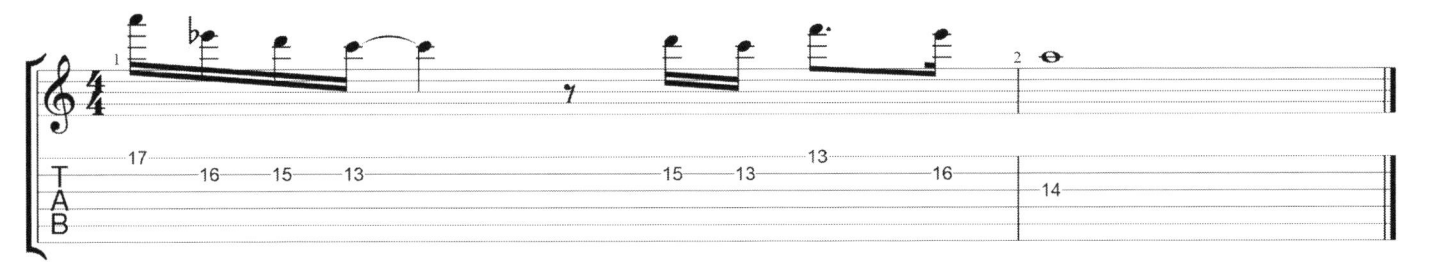

Example 5 | Track 76

This example is resolving to the b6th.

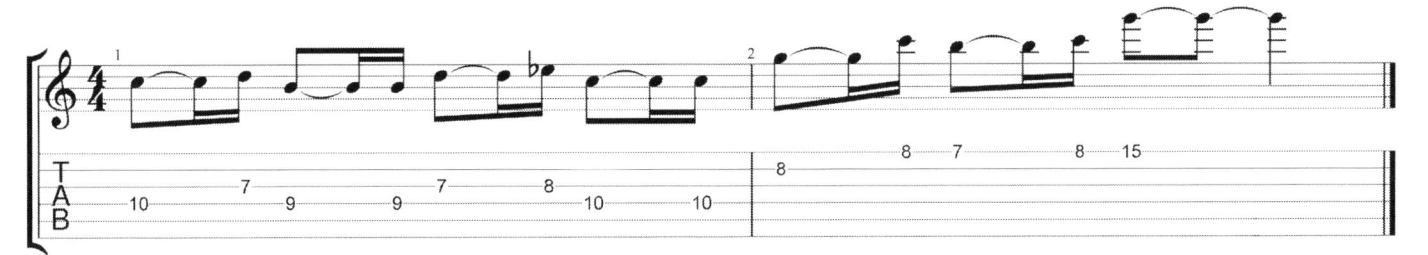

Example 6 | Track 77

Here we are resolving to the b7th.

Below are some examples of the #9 'sweet note':

Example 7 | Track 78

This is resolving to the b6th.

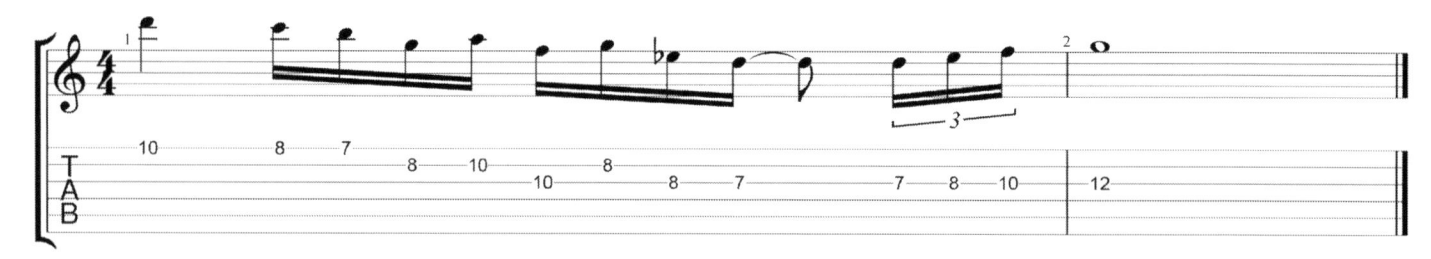

Example 8 | Track 79

Here we are resolving to the b7th.

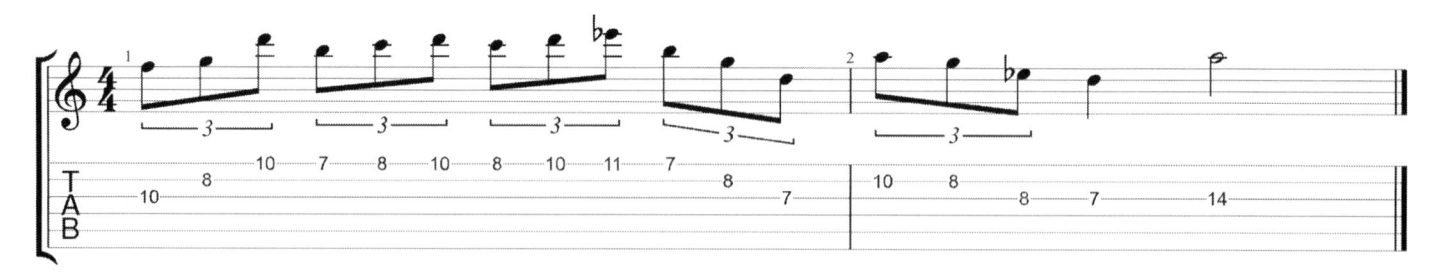

Example 9 | Track 80

This example is resolving to the b7th.

Next are some examples of the #11 'sweet note':

Example 10 | Track 81

This is resolving to the b2nd.

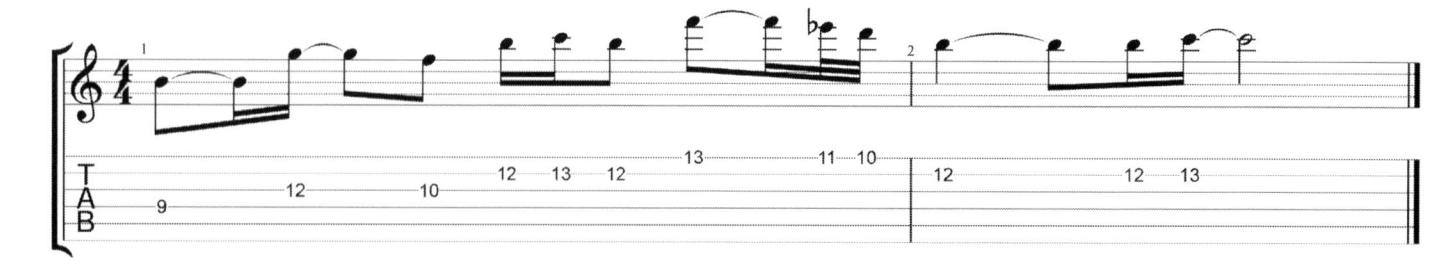

Example 11 | Track 82

Here we are resolving to the b4th. (Enharmonically this is a major 3rd)

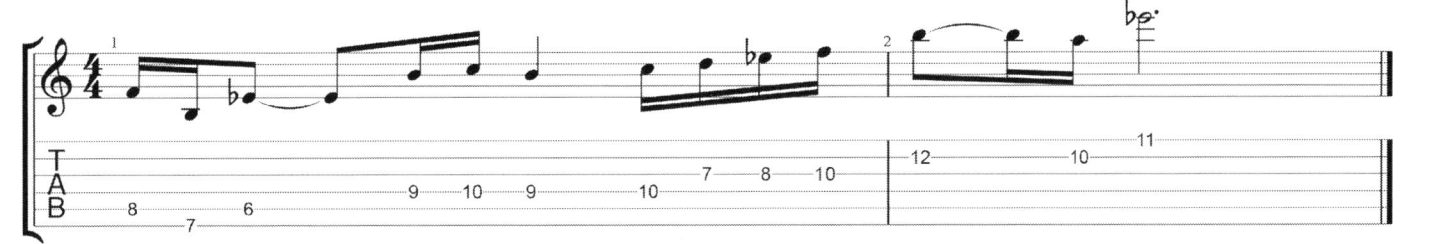

Example 12 | Track 83

This is resolving to the b7th.

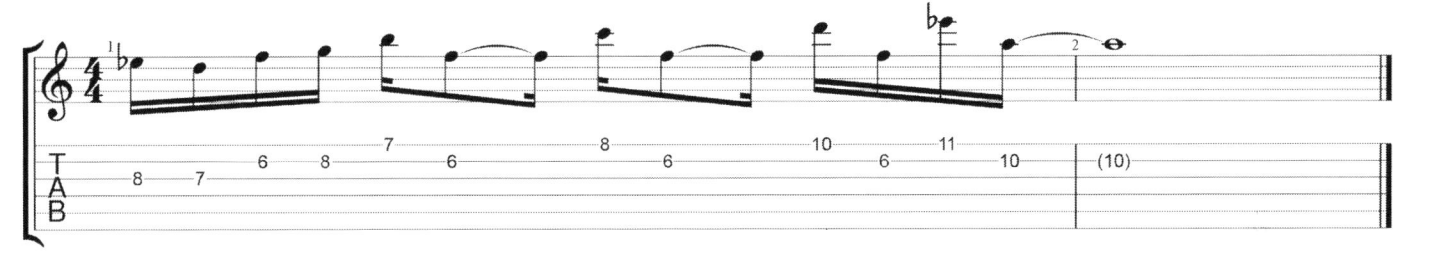

Beneath are some examples of the b13 'sweet note':

Example 13 | Track 84

Here we are resolving to the b7th.

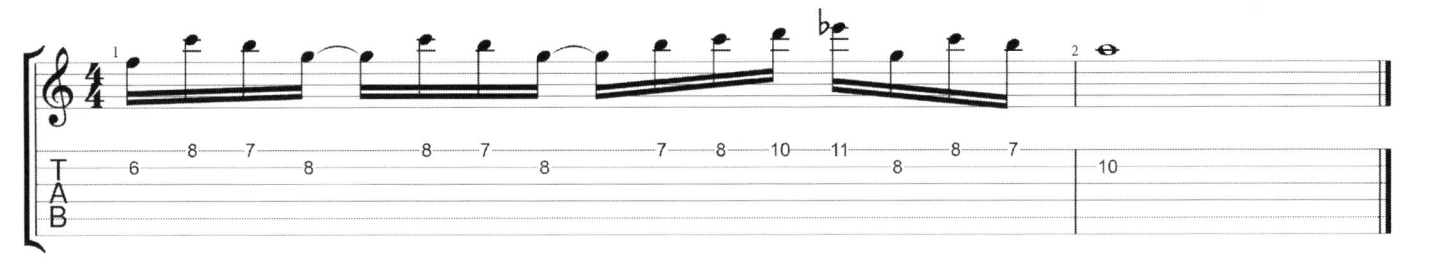

Example 14 | Track 85

This example is resolving to the b3rd.

Example 15 | Track 86

This is resolving to the b3rd.

Food For Thought

If you were to target the #9 'sweet note' over a V7 chord, that V7 chord would become a V7#9 chord. Likewise, if you were to target the b13 'sweet note', the V7 chord would become a V7b13 chord.

Apply It To Your Style

Now that you're beginning to the grasp the Super Locrian mode, it's time to integrate it into your playing. In these examples we are focusing on one 'sweet note' at a time. We recommend you do the same when writing your own lines. This way you will clearly define an altered tension over a V7 chord, rather than trying to do too many things at once.

Here are some examples of the B Super Locrian mode to be played over the standard rock backing track:

Example 16 | Track 87

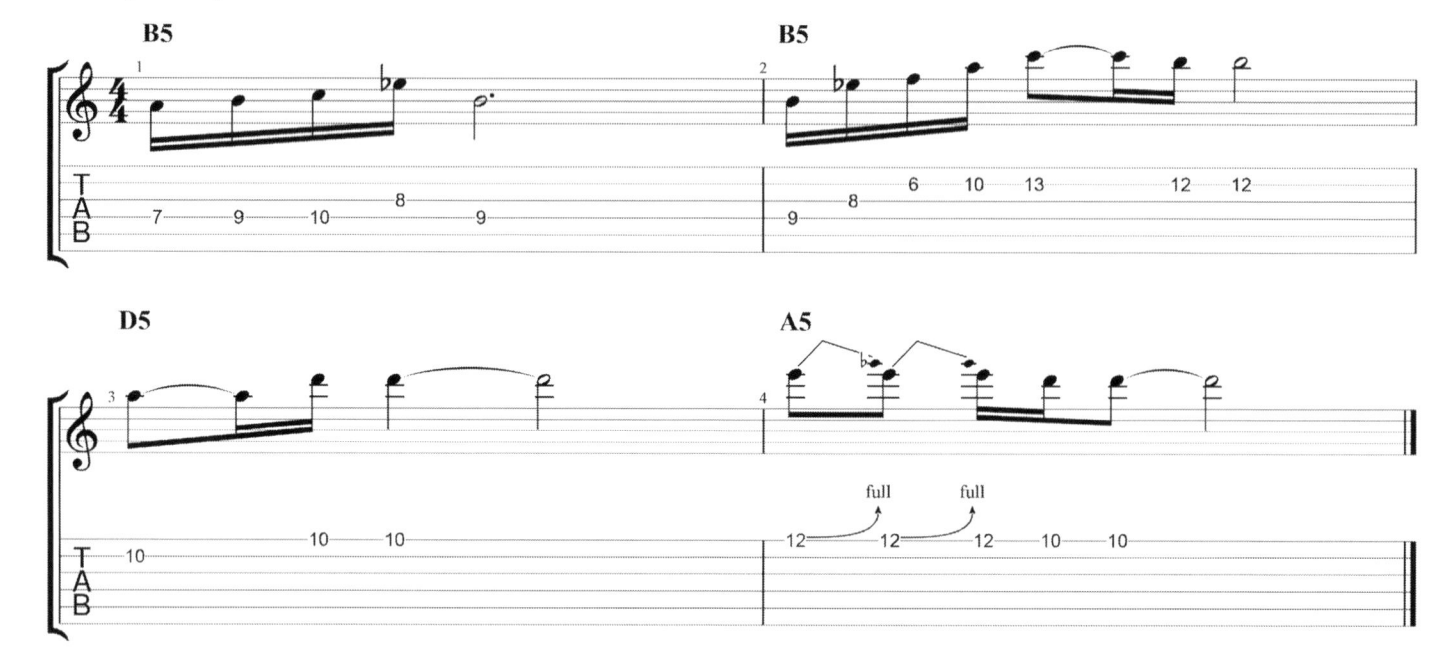

Example 17 | Track 88

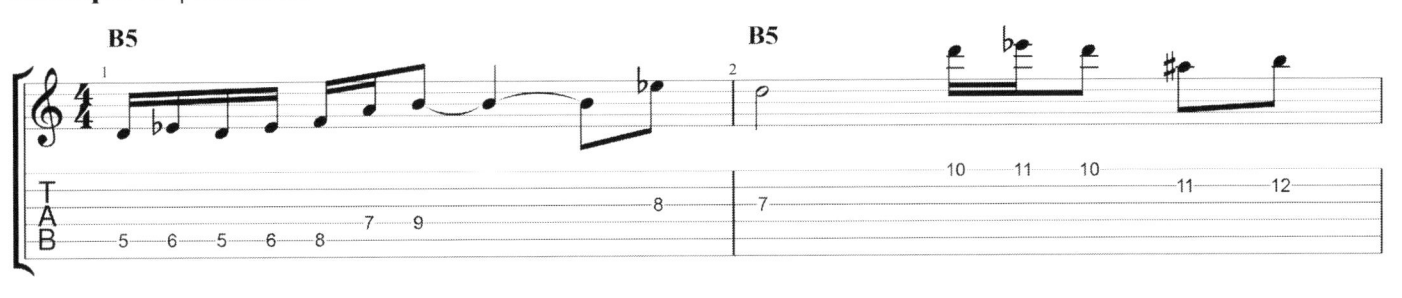

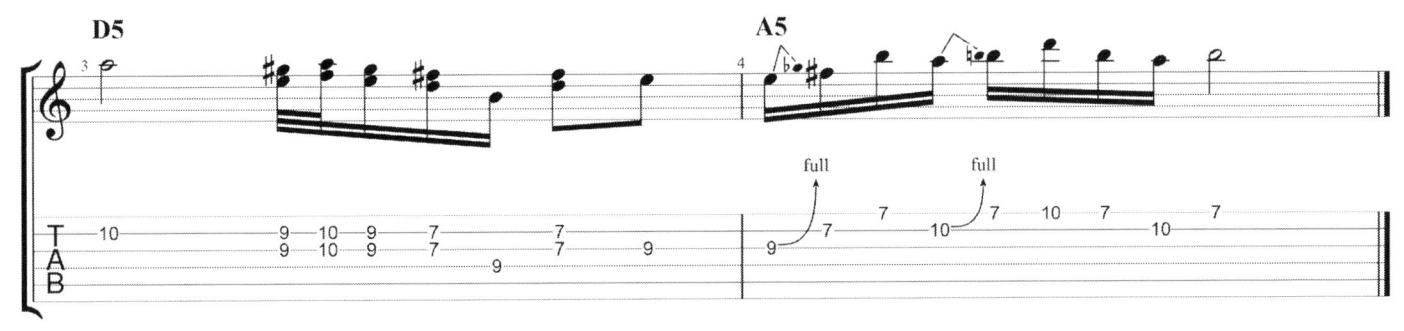

Example 18 | Track 89

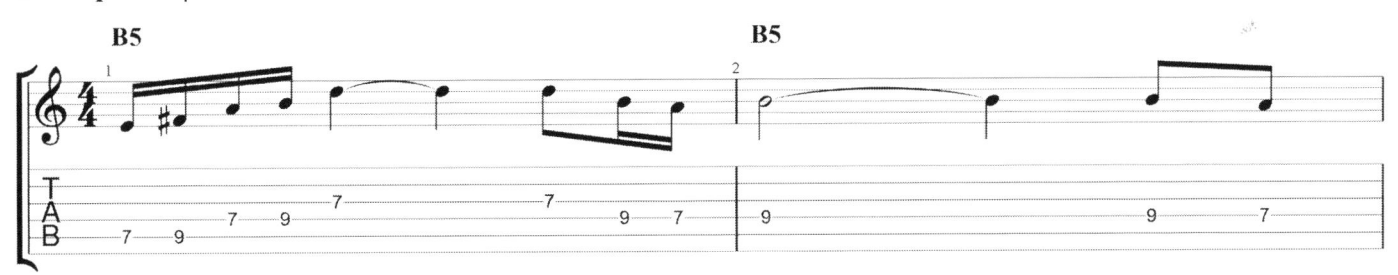

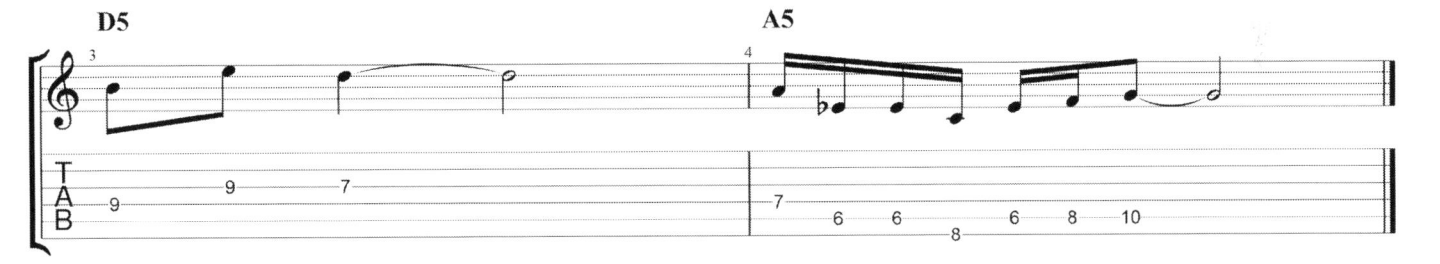

63

Example 19 | Track 90

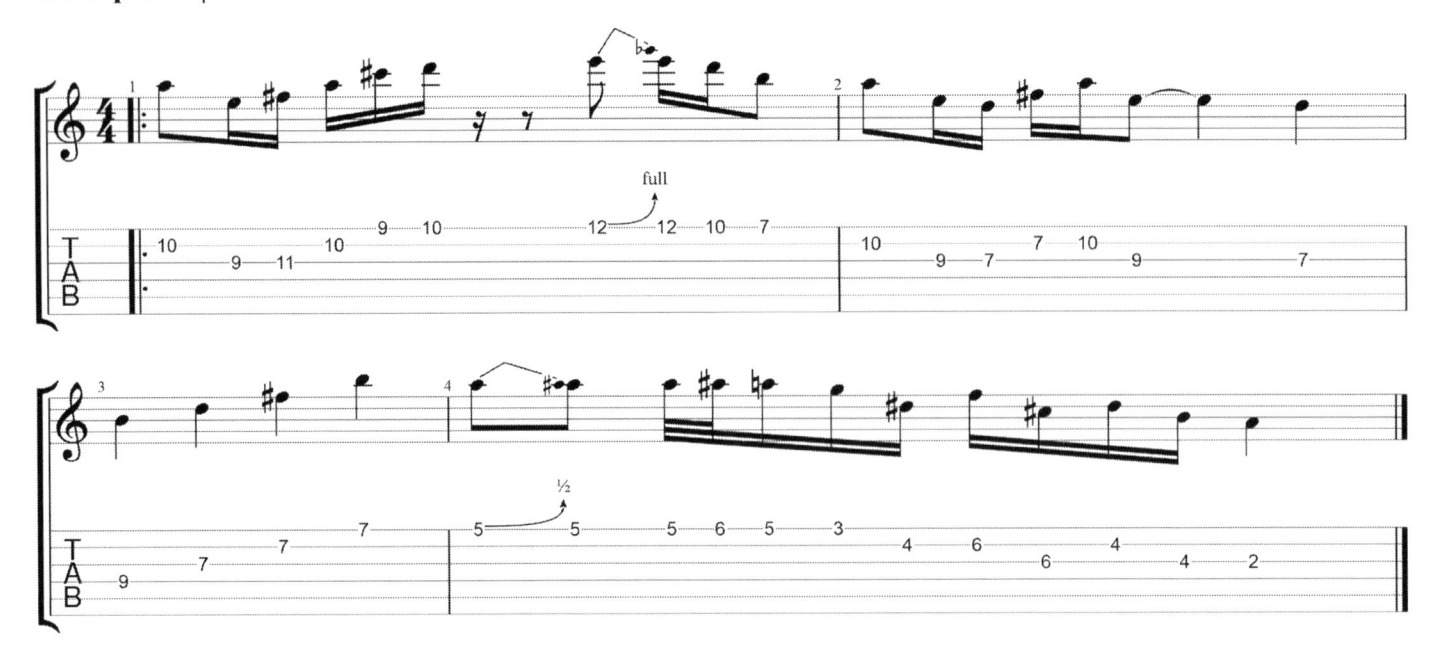

Now that you have another mode under your belt, add it to the sequence of modes to practice.

Remember to revisit content from previous chapters. You will find many similarities between each mode. You may even find that a previous chapter will help you understand some confusing aspects of a different mode you may be stuck on. Keep practicing and building up your own style of playing over the backing tracks provided.

How Do We Use This?

Now that you've been introduced to the seven modes of Melodic Minor it's time to take it a little further. You may be asking yourself, "how can I apply this to real situations?" To help you answer this question, we have put together backing tracks and example solos to demonstrate how we would use these modes in context. We recommend learning the solos to get familiar with the tracks, and working in your own ideas over the same backing tracks. It would be a good idea to keep referring back to previous chapters to reinforce your knowledge of these modes and their applications.

Example 1 | Track 91

Soul Funk

66

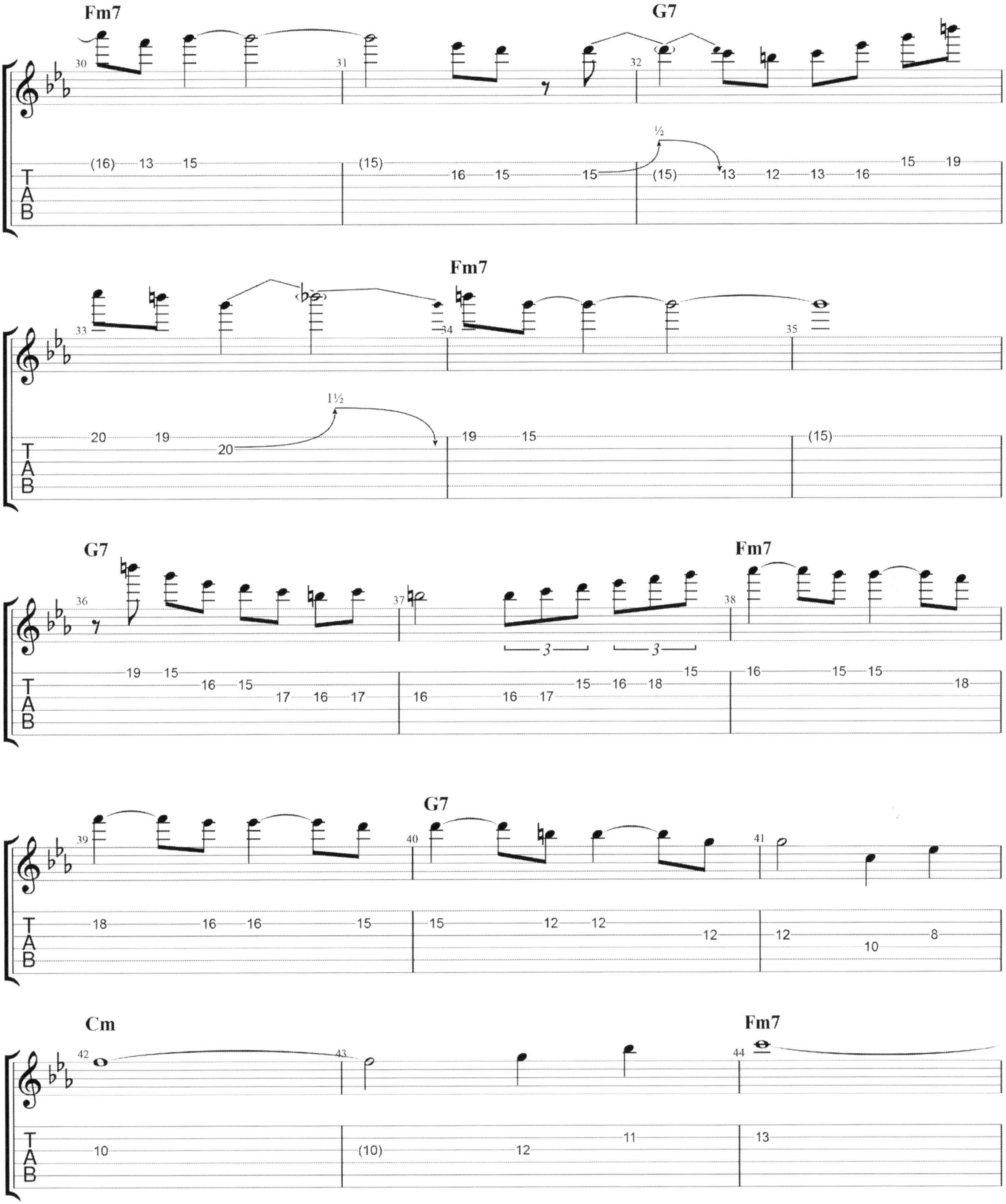
Fm7
G7
Fm7
G7
Fm7
G7
Cm
Fm7

68

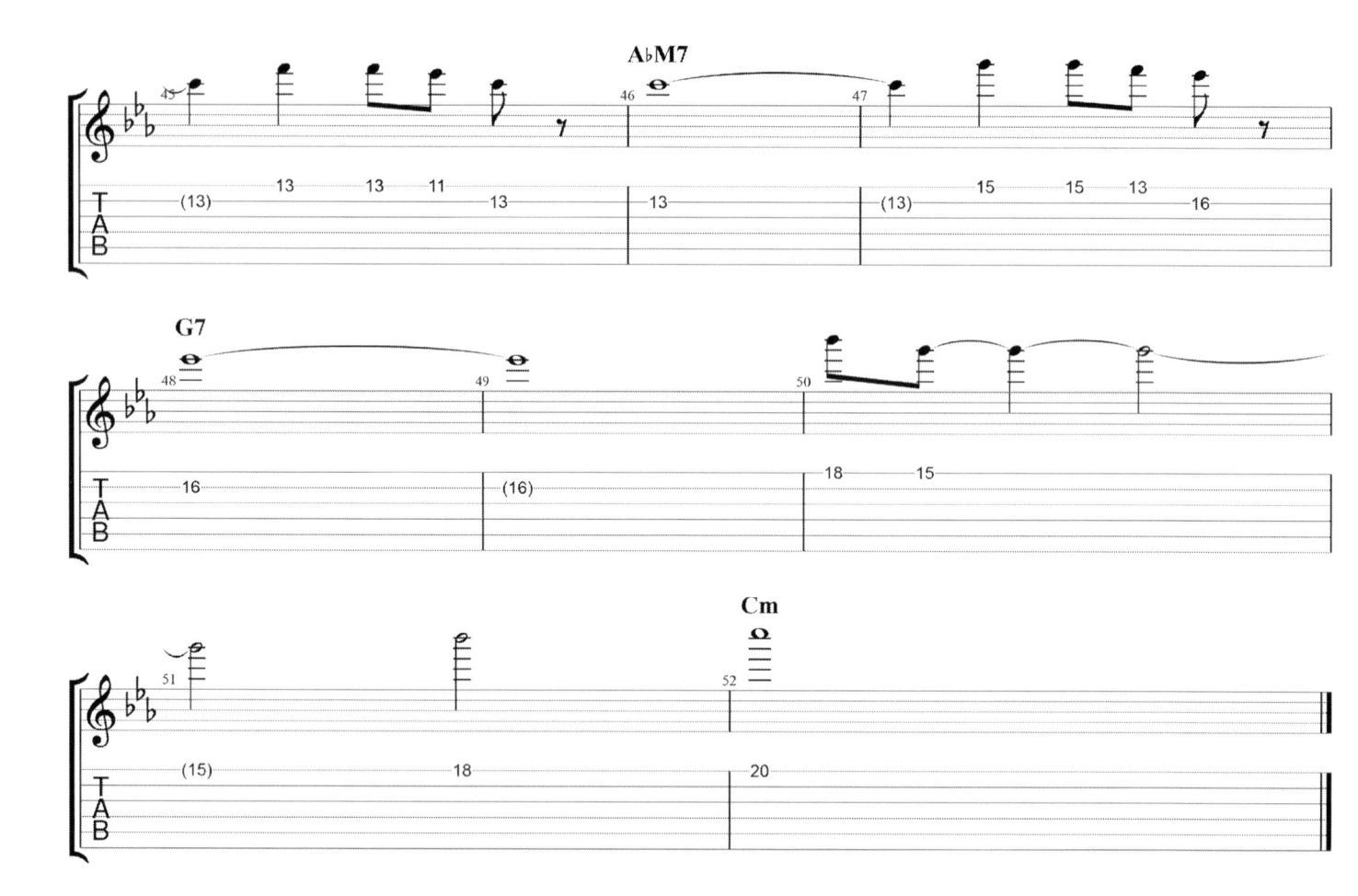

Example 2 | Track 93
Heavy Metal

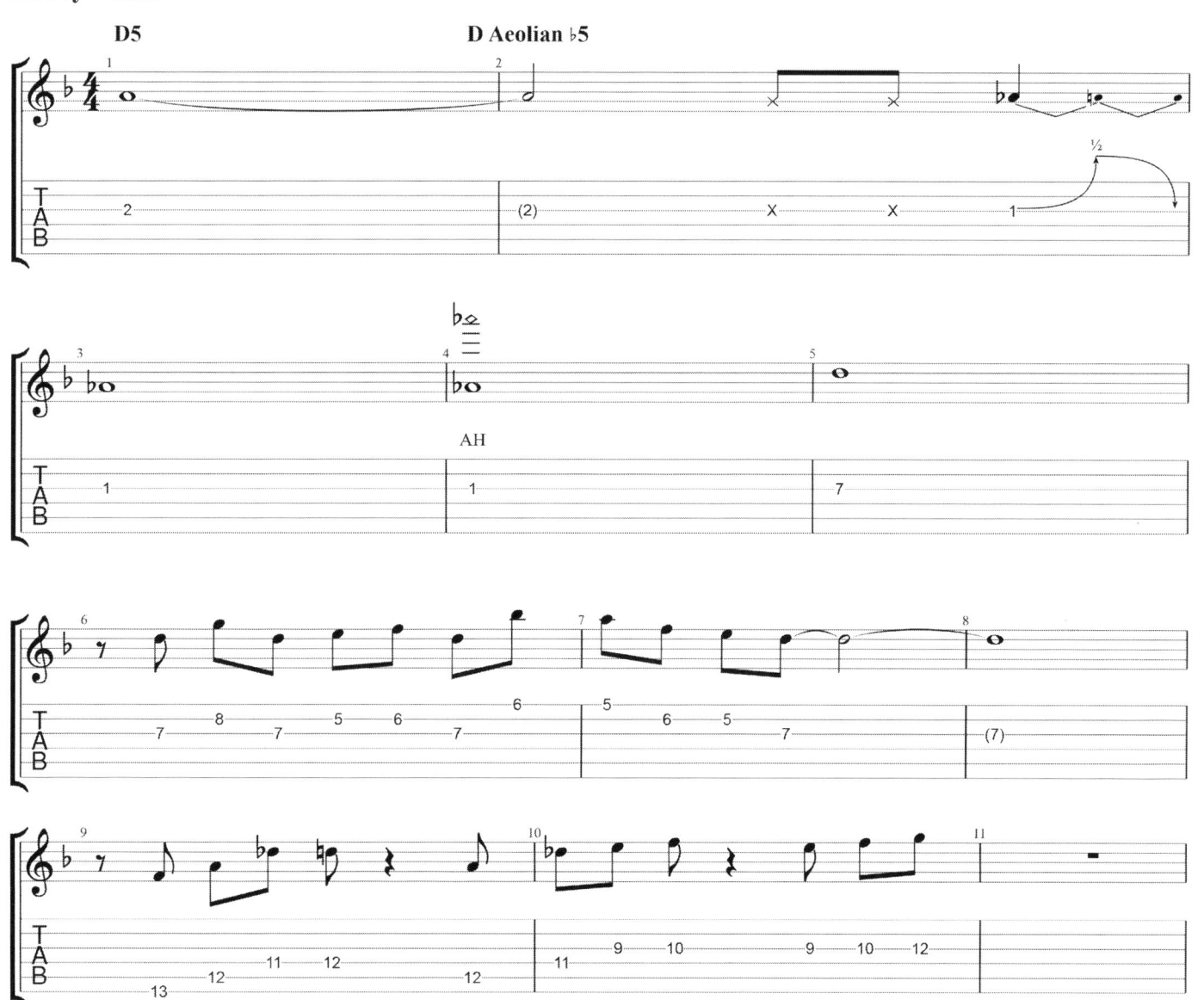

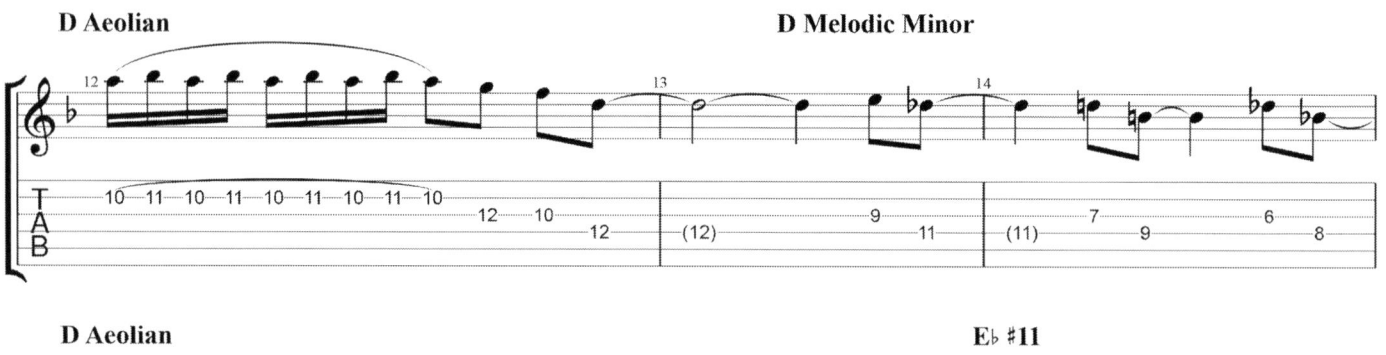

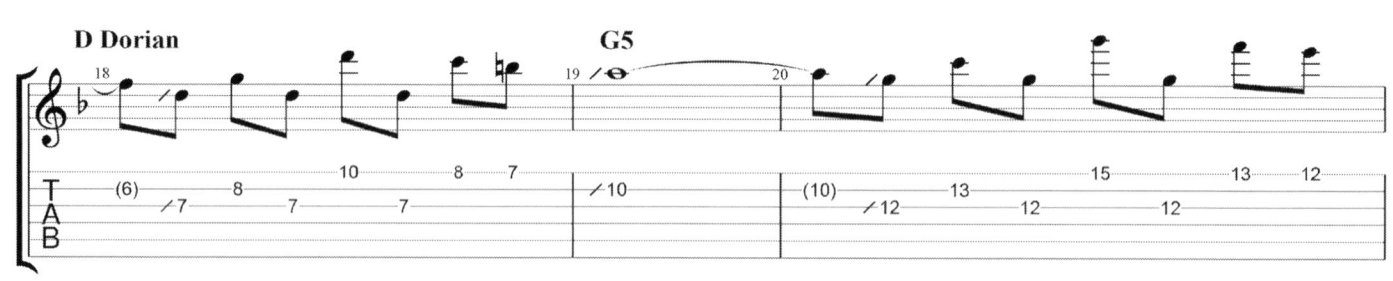

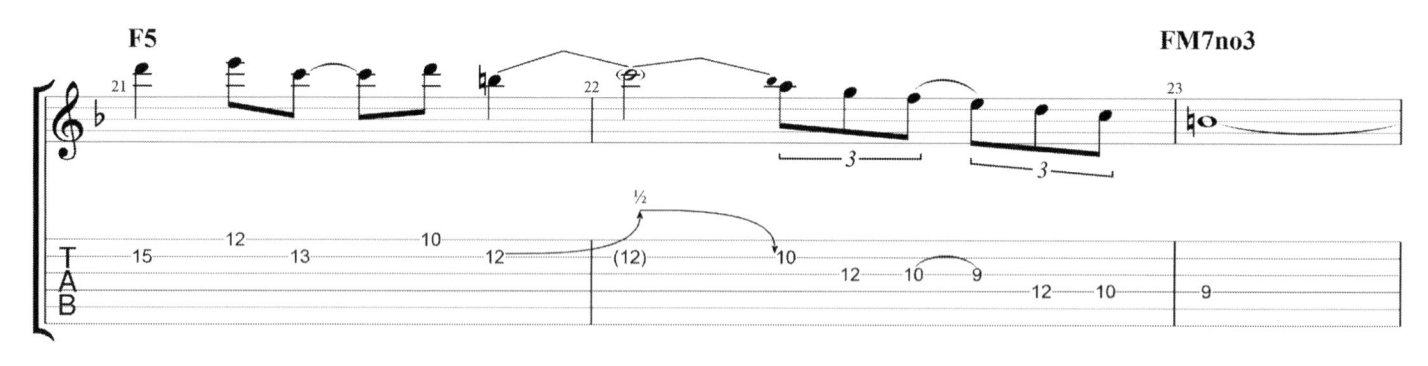

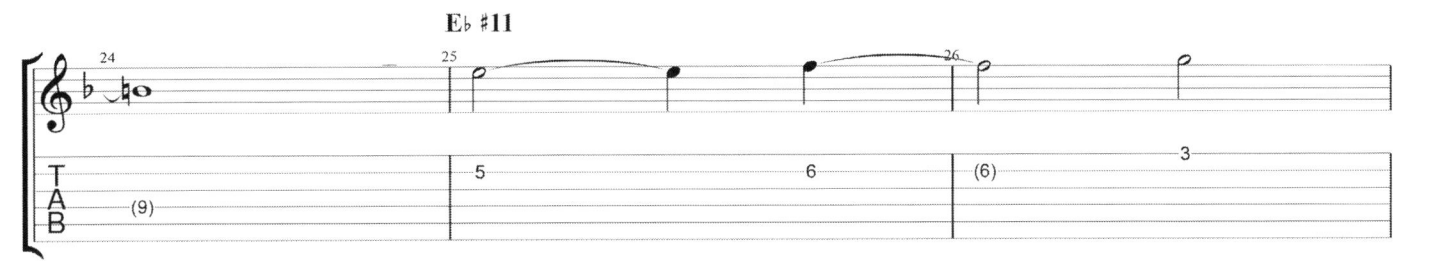

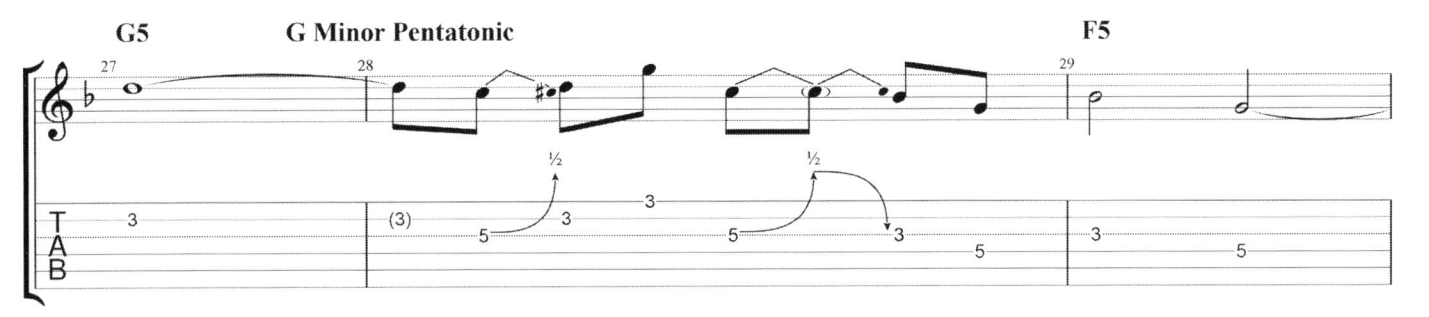

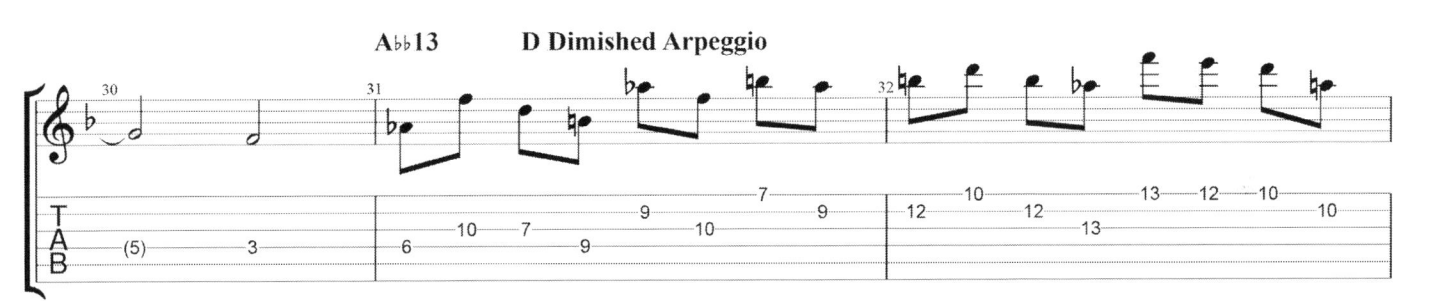

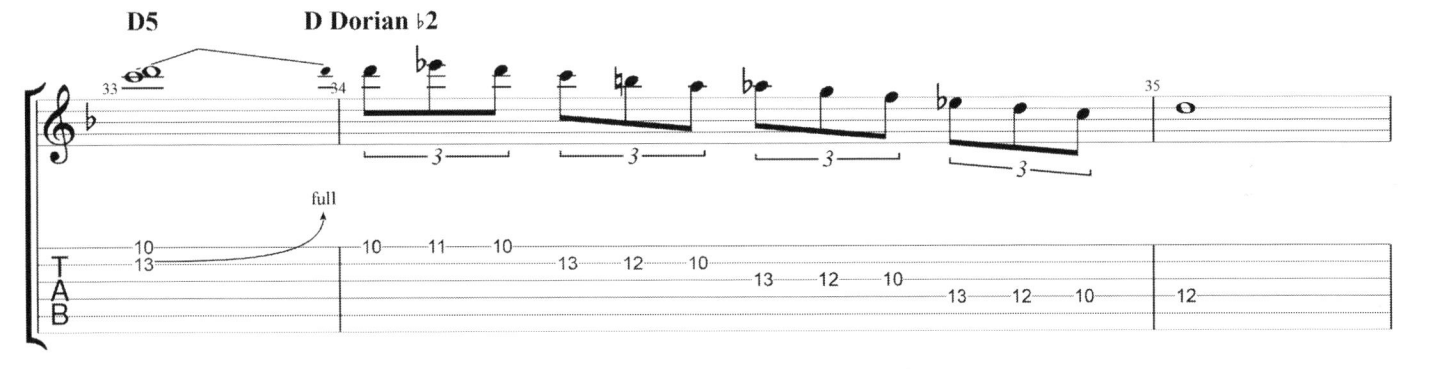

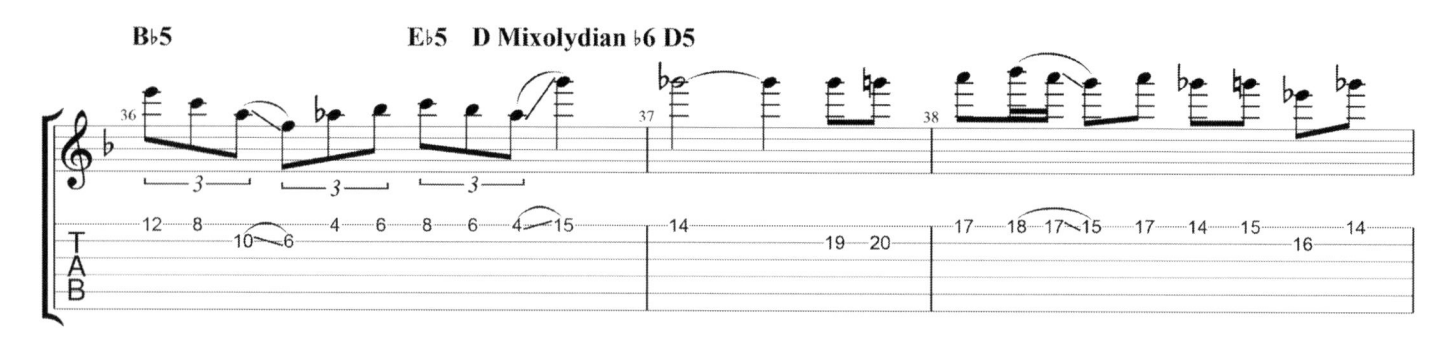

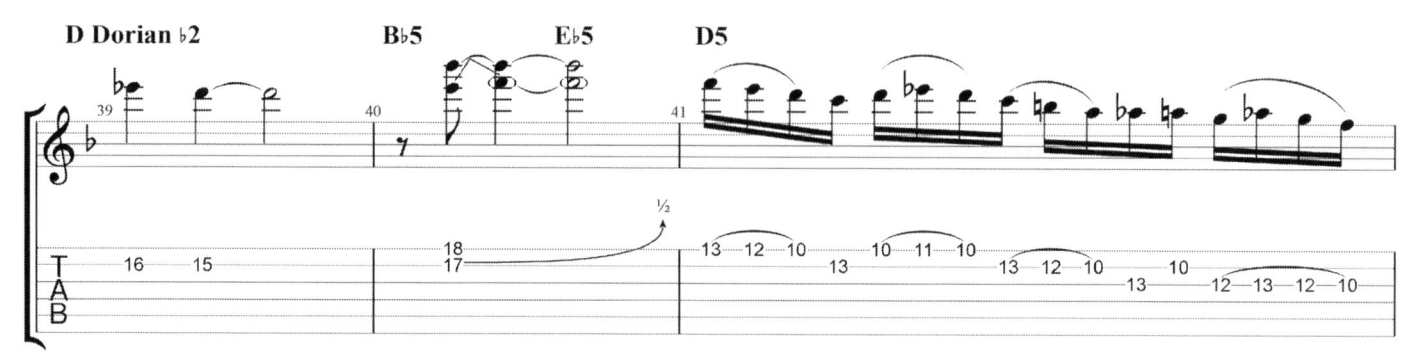

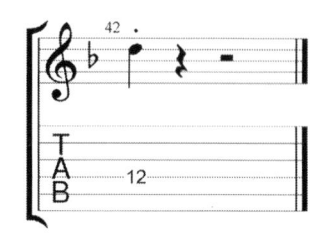

Example 3 | Track 95

Power Rock

A
A Minor Pentatonic
G
D
A
A Melodic Minor
E
E Super Locrian
E7 #9
A
A Dorian
full
½
G
D
A
full
full
G
D
full

Example 4 | Track 97

Hair Rock

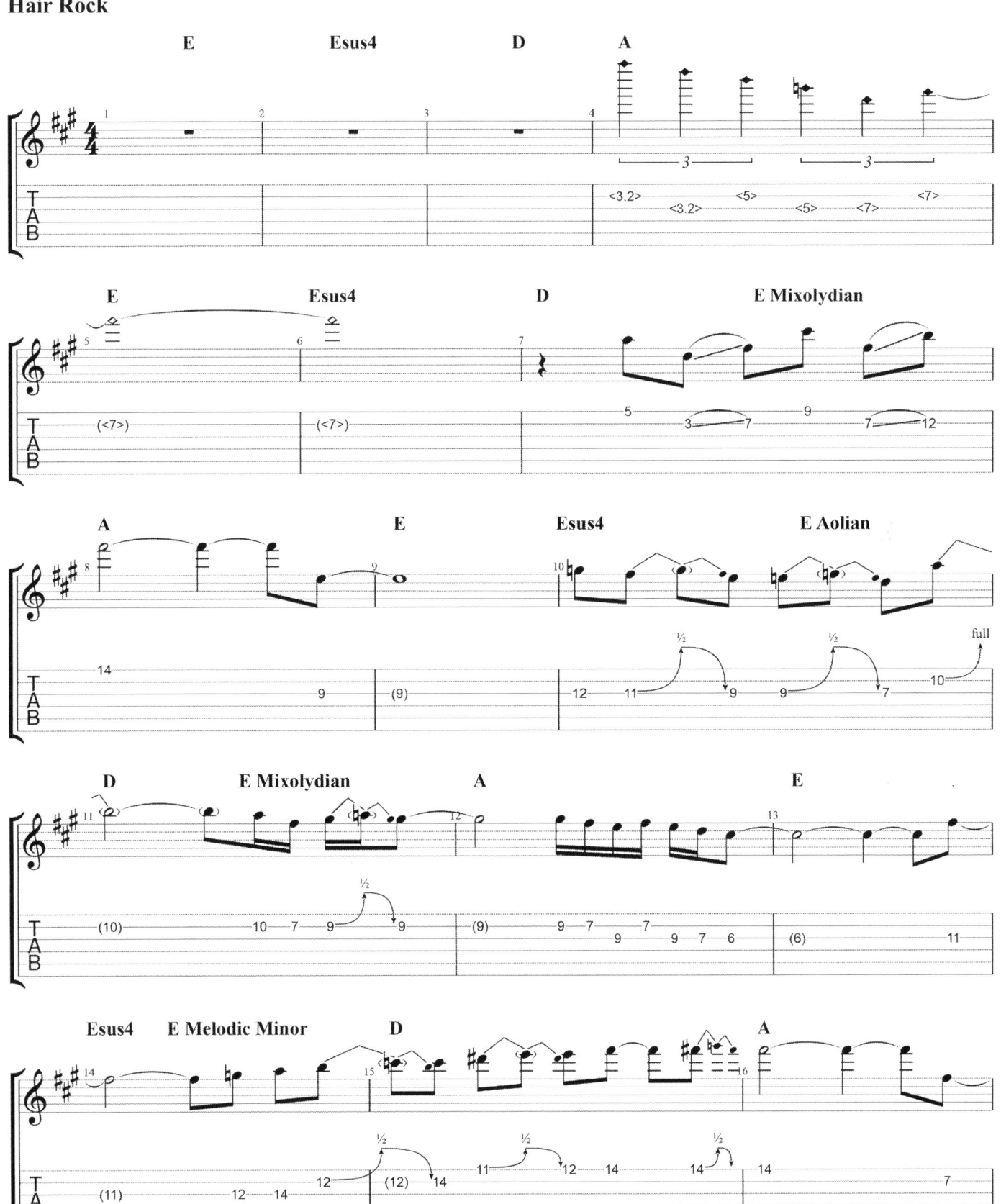

F♯m7
E Mixolydian
E5
E Mixolydian ♭6
½
½
F♯m7
E Mixolydian
E5
E Mixolydian ♭6
F♯m7
E Mixolydian
E5
E Dorian ♭2
full
full
G5
A5
full

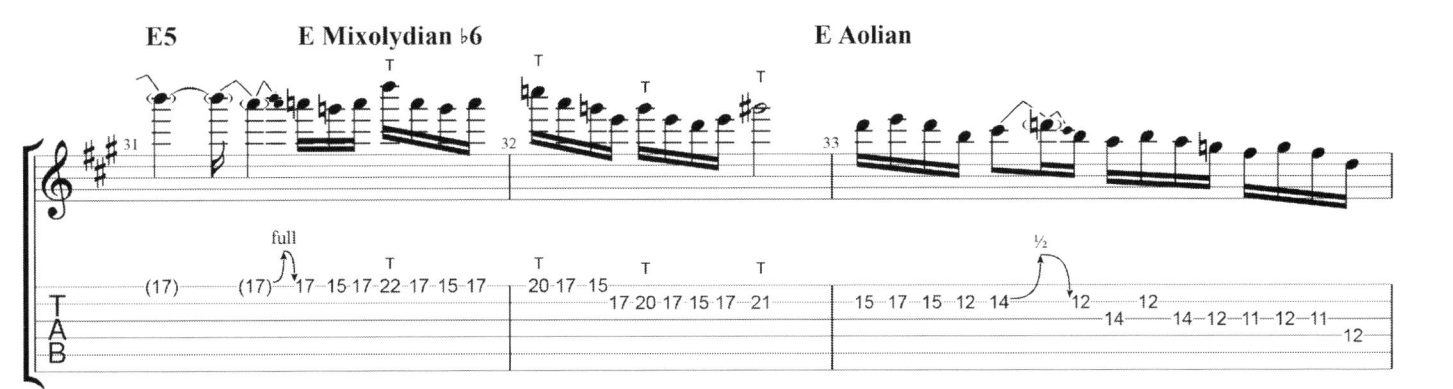

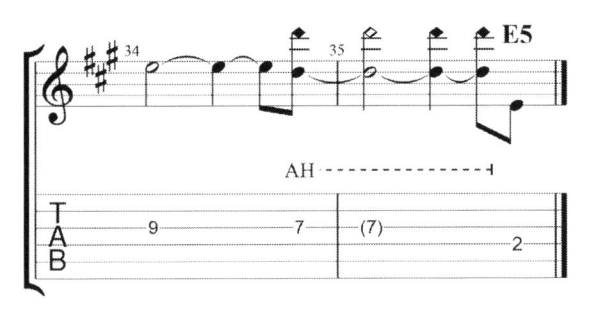

Further Reading

While this book is a good starting point, it is by no means the definitive text on Melodic Minor. We found these sources really helpful when writing this book. We recommend that you check them out as they will further your understanding of the Melodic Minor modes and their applications.

Berle, A. (1994) *Patterns, Scales & Modes for Jazz Guitar*, Logan, IA: Amsco Publications.

Fewell, G. (2005) Jazz Improvization for Guitar: A Melodic Approach, Boston, MA: Berklee Press.

Fewell, G. (2010) *Jazz Improvization for Guitar*, Boston, MA: Berklee Press.

Greene, T. (1981) *Jazz Guitar: Single Note Soloing*, Vol.1, Van Nuys, CA: Belwin-Mills Publishing Corp.

Levine, M. (1995) *The Jazz Theory Book, Petaluma*, CA: Sher Music Company.

Pease, T. and Pullig, K. (2001) *Modern Jazz Voicings*, Boston, MA: Berklee Press.

Ricker, R. (1999) The Developing Improviser: The Melodic Minor Scale Vol.Four, Rottenburg: Advance Music.

Slonimsky, N. (1975) *Thesaurus of Scales and Melodic Patterns*, New York, NY: Charles Scribner's Sons.

Steinel, M. (1995) *Building A Jazz Vocabulary*, Milwaukee, WI: Hal Leonard Corporation.

Tagliarino, B. (2012) Harmonic Minor, Melodic Minor and Diminished Scales for Guitar, United Kingdom: Behemoth Publishers.

Weiskopf, W. (2000) *Around The Horn*, New Albany, IN:Jamey Aebersold Jazz, Inc.

Printed in Great Britain
by Amazon